Crafting for Good
Feng Shui

Crafting for Good
Feng Shui

40 PROJECTS TO BRING HARMONY TO YOUR HOME

JANICE EATON KILBY WITH A FOREWORD BY MASTER PETER LEUNG

LARK BOOKS

A Division of Sterling Publishing Co., Inc.
New York

Author:
JANICE EATON KILBY

Art Director:
DANA MARGARET IRWIN

Photographer:
SANDRA STAMBAUGH

Cover Designer:
BARBARA ZARETSKY

Illustrator:
ORRIN LUNDGREN

Assistant Editor:
RAIN NEWCOMB

Assistant Art Director:
HANNES CHAREN

Production Assistance:
SHANNON YOKELEY,
LORELEI BUCKLEY

Editorial Assistance:
DELORES GOSNELL

Library of Congress Cataloging-in-Publication Data

Kilby, Janice Eaton, 1955-
   Crafting for good Feng Shui : 40 projects to bring harmony to your home / Janice Eaton Kilby ; with a foreword by Peter Leung.—1st ed.
      p. cm.
   ISBN 1-57990-364-9 (paper)
   1. Feng shui. I. Title.

 BF1779.F4 K485 2003
 133.3'337—dc21

2002028788

10 9 8 7 6 5 4 3 2 1

First Edition

Published by Lark Books, a division of
Sterling Publishing Co., Inc.
387 Park Avenue South, New York, N.Y. 10016

© 2003, Lark Books

Distributed in Canada by Sterling Publishing,
c/o Canadian Manda Group, One Atlantic Ave., Suite 105
Toronto, Ontario, Canada M6K 3E7

Distributed in the U.K. by Guild of Master Craftsman Publications Ltd., Castle Place,
166 High Street, Lewes, East Sussex, England
BN7 1XU
Tel: (+ 44) 1273 477374, Fax: (+ 44) 1273 478606, Email: pubs@thegmcgroup.com,
Web: www.gmcpublications.com

Distributed in Australia by Capricorn Link (Australia) Pty Ltd.,
P.O. Box 704, Windsor, NSW 2756 Australia

If you have questions or comments about this book, please contact:
Lark Books
67 Broadway
Asheville, NC 28801
(828) 236-9730

Printed in China

ISBN 1-57990-364-9

CONTENTS

FOREWORD

Feng Shui is about life and, to many people, life is unpredictable. It's full of ups and downs, successes and failures, and changes we can't explain. In good times, we find ourselves blessed by success at work and happy family relationships. Things go well for us and our loved ones, and life is good. But sometimes we get sick, lose our jobs, suffer financial reverses, or experience strife in our relationships. Sometimes this happens after moving into a new home. Sometimes, instead of a major catastrophe, we experience a nonstop stream of difficulties. Nothing seems to come easily.

Is it possible to foresee problems and head them off? To live our lives in ease and harmony? Yes! And I believe you can do it by practicing good Feng Shui.

Feng Shui is a study of the human living environment and how it affects our lives. It's simple, profound, and effective when done correctly. It's not a religion, it's not superstition, and you don't need to be a rocket scientist to practice it. You can train yourself to see with Feng Shui eyes and sharpen your Feng Shui awareness through careful observation of your surroundings over a period of time. Once you know how to look, you'll understand how to encourage good things to come to you and your family. Or you'll be able to pinpoint sources of difficulty in your life and change them, too, making room for happiness and good fortune to emerge.

Crafting for Good Feng Shui by Janice Eaton Kilby outlines the basic ideas underlying good Feng Shui and contains many simple and ingenious suggestions for creating a home filled with beauty, peace, and harmony. It covers the different aspects and traditions of Feng Shui including the most ancient, called Form School. That is my own tradition and training. I have practiced Form School Feng Shui for the past 30 years, and my research and work with other people have shown time and again that our health, wealth, and family happiness can be greatly affected by the exterior landscape and interior architectural design of our home.

As Feng Shui grows in popularity in the West, I believe it's extremely important to bring fundamental Form School knowledge to the general public so well-intentioned beginners experience positive instead of harmful results. You'll read about many of these issues, and get useful answers, in *Crafting for Good Feng Shui*.

Are you ready to approach Feng Shui with an open, logical, and investigative mind? If so, you're ready to experience how fascinating and potent Feng Shui can be. *Crafting for Good Feng Shui* will help you get started.

Master Peter Leung
www.fengshuisos.com
Toronto, Canada

INTRODUCTION

Like so many wisdom traditions from faraway places and times that have made their way to the West, Feng Shui attracts more interest every day. Since it began in China thousands of years ago, this ancient practice is beautifully represented by its Chinese ideograms, which literally translate as *wind* and *water*.

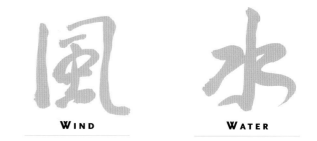

WIND   **WATER**

Perhaps you're intrigued by the people who testify that Feng Shui has improved their personal well-being, their relationships, and their careers. Or, you may simply want to enjoy living in an attractive home that not only looks wonderful but *feels* good because it's organized and decorated according to Feng Shui principles.

Feng Shui is mystical, but it's not a religion. It's poetic, but it's also full of common sense. It's an art, but it's also very practical and results-oriented. It's a method of siting, designing, furnishing, organizing, and decorating your home with the purpose of obtaining concrete, positive effects in important areas of your life.

Crafting for Good Feng Shui explains the basics of this ancient art and shows how easy it is to make beautiful things to fit your modern lifestyle and create good energy around you. You don't have to retrofit your home to resemble Old China, although Asian imagery may work beautifully within your decorating scheme. It's your choice!

Except for a very few cases, it's also not necessary to make major structural changes in your home to conform with Feng Shui principles. There are plenty of less demanding solutions, and this book shows you how to make objects and use materials, shapes, and colors to affect your home's energies in a positive fashion, attracting good and eliminating bad energy. Chapter one explains the essence of Feng Shui and how to use its most important tools. Chapter two reviews Feng Shui problems commonly found in Western homes and gives easy solutions, and chapter three features a real-life, room-by-room makeover of a house. Finally, chapter four includes dozens of gorgeous how-to projects to help you improve all aspects of your life.

You can utilize Feng Shui effectively at many different levels, and it does *not* require complex astronomical calculations, mind-boggling charts, or rigid adherence to dozens of complicated rules, so relax! While many people seek the seasoned counsel of Feng Shui masters, who have spent their entire lives understanding the subtleties of the art and perfecting their skills, Feng Shui can be practiced at many levels and there is no one, perfect way to do it.

As you become familiar with the basic principles of Feng Shui, you'll develop greater sensitivity to the nuances of your environment. You'll be able to analyze how the layout and contents of your home may be affecting the quality of your life, and you can start to make some helpful changes right away.

Crafting for Good Feng Shui is designed so you can select among beautiful how-to projects to blend in

WITH AN EYE MADE QUIET BY THE POWER OF HARMONY, AND THE DEEP POWER OF JOY, WE SEE INTO THE LIFE OF THINGS.

William Wordsworth,
Lines Composed a Few Miles Above Tintern Abbey

with your lifestyle and provide the harmonious, balanced energies that make your home a healing place and serene refuge. Most important, you'll learn to trust your own preferences, feelings, and intuition about what works for you and your family.

So what are you waiting for? Turn the page and get ready to enjoy the wonderful things to come in your life.

Above: *A couple wishing to enhance the quality of their relationship might add romantic imagery, sensual colors, and pairs of objects to their bedroom.*

Below: *This living room incorporates earthy colors, natural materials, and open space suitable for a home's center.*

The Essence of Feng Shui

to understand Feng Shui (fung SHWAY) it's necessary to set aside our modern way of looking at things and to understand the worldview of the ancient Chinese. Energy, harmony, and balance were—and continue to be—key concepts. But there are other important ideas and tools used in Feng Shui, too, and you've probably heard of some of them. Once you understand how they operate and interact, you'll be equipped to apply the wonderful art of Feng Shui to your home with confidence. They include:

- Taoism (DOW-iz-im)

- *Chi* (CHEE), the universal energy

- *Yin* and *Yang*

- The *I Ching* (EEE JING) and the eight trigrams

- The directions of the compass

- The Five Elements of Fire, Water, Wood, Metal, and Earth

- The Form School and Compass School of Feng Shui

- The *bagua* (BAH-gwah), a diagram which literally maps the energy sectors within a space and the important aspects of our lives affected by each sector

GOOD FORTUNE SYMBOLISM

Chinese culture produced a very rich symbolic language, and Feng Shui uses many symbols, often flowers and animals, to attract good fortune, wealth, and longevity. For example, a peony flower may represent the presence of a young, unmarried woman in a household, thereby attracting an eligible suitor, while a fish or frog brings prosperity. You'll see many of these images and objects as you page through this book.

The numbers 7, 8, and 9 are considered particularly lucky by the Chinese. This is due largely to the "Like attracts like" philosophy that permeates Feng Shui. For example, the Chinese pronunciation of the number 8 sounds very much like the words for

CONTINUED ON PAGE 12

GOOD FORTUNE SYMBOLISM
CONTINUED FROM PAGE 11

"increased wealth." Number 9 is favored due to its mysterious arithmetical powers: Try multiplying 9 by any number from 1 to 10, then adding the digits of the resulting number. For example, 4 times 9 equals 36, and 3 plus 6 equals. . .9! Or, 5 times 9 equals 45, and 4 plus 5 equals. . . you guessed it! On the other hand, the number 4 is extremely inauspicious and to be avoided, and 5 isn't so great either.

The double fish symbol attracts good luck, and many Chinese restaurants position large aquariums in front to enhance revenues.

The double happiness symbol is a well-known and much-beloved activator of good family fortune.

CHI, TAOISM, AND THE ORIGINS OF FENG SHUI

Since ancient times, the Chinese philosophy called Taoism has held that the universe consists of flows of energy which affect the world and everything in it. Likewise, we are surrounded, molded, and permeated by this flowing, invisible energy known as chi. Equally important, that energy always seeks balance between opposites: activity versus stillness, light versus dark.

Interior of Taoist temple on Hong Kong Island, China.
Image by Jon Bower at www.apexphotos.com

Inspired by Taoism, the underlying concepts of Feng Shui began to take form in the writings of ninth-century imperial advisor Yang Yun Sang. Yang wrote that one could examine the shapes of mountains, rivers, and valleys to locate the auspicious energies symbolized by the celestial animals called the Green Dragon and White Tiger. By capturing and harnessing the dragon's cosmic breath, which Yang called chi, one obtained good fortune.

ILLUSTRATION BY HANS-GEORG STRUNZ.
COURTESY OF THE FENG SHUI CENTER SWITZERLAND

Form school Feng shui

Yang's writings formed the basis of the *Form* (or *Landform*) *School* of Feng Shui. The dragon remains the principal symbol of Feng Shui, and it and the three other Celestial Creatures—the White Tiger, Crimson Phoenix, and Black Turtle—are very powerful good luck symbols. Today's Form School practitioners study cityscapes and suburbs as well as landscapes to determine the most auspicious location of buildings and other structures and the location of paths of energy on the earth's surface called dragon veins.

Popularity of Form school in the West

Many westerners today prefer the easy-to-understand Form School practices of using the location of the front door, and the main door of each room, to help them analyze the energies inside their homes. This method is explained below in Orienting the Aspects of Life Bagua (page 25). Even Compass School adherents use Form School methods to correct energies outside a home first before correcting the Feng Shui inside.

Coins tied with red cord or ribbon are traditionally used to activate wealth luck. Round with a square opening in the middle, a Chinese coin represents the auspicious combination of heaven and earth. The side with four Chinese characters is the yang side, and the yin side contains two. Hang a strand of coins yang side out on the doorknob outside your front door and see what happens.

The silver dollar plant (*Lunaria annua*), also called the money plant, is a wealth attractor, and placing lush, live plants in the southeast sector of a home also activates prosperity luck.

The three deities Fuk, Luk, and Sau (left to right) are displayed in most Chinese households, sometimes as life-sized statues in the main entrance of a home. They represent and attract wealth (Fuk), health (Luk), and long life (Sau).

More About Form School

The sheer variety and beauty of names for natural and man-made landscapes give a clue to how complex and subtle Form School Feng Shui can be. Landforms resembling animals, especially dragons, are considered very powerful. "Golden Dragon Coiled around Flower" and "Baby Dragon Looking at Its Mother" are two of the many names for rare mountain formations which produce extraordinary people and events. Very flat land or, at the other extreme, threatening or jagged landforms are regarded as inauspicious. Gentle, rippling bodies of water or earth-sprung sources such as streams and creeks are preferable to fierce coastlines or raging rivers.

Compass School Feng Shui

In the centuries following the genesis of Form School, the *Li Chi* (LEE CHEE) School (Theory of Chi School) arose. Today, it is known as Compass School. Form School and Compass School agree on several basic ideas, including the concept of chi and how it moves. They also concur that there are two major types of energy called yin and yang. And finally, they share the concepts of the Five Elements and the eight trigrams of the I Ching. All of these ideas are explained below.

Compass School Feng Shui is based on the idea that the eight directions of the compass literally possess different types of energy and therefore the different directions of a room contain different energies. Compass School is also very black-and-white, right or wrong. The measurements of a table height or the direction your bed faces, for example, are either good or bad for you; there's no in-between. Compass School analyzes in great detail a person's birth date, birth year, and the relative location of stars. If you like working with very specific rules and/or astrological and numerological calculations, you may wish to explore this type of Feng Shui. There are many excellent, exhaustive books on the subject. Refer to the section Recommended Reading, on page 158.

Whatever tradition of Feng Shui you follow, once you've analyzed your home's Feng Shui and decided what you'd like to improve, this book shows how to make objects in the proper materials, shapes, and colors to adjust your home's energies—and where to position them to evade or dispel bad chi and attract good chi.

Above: *Image by Jon Bower at www.apexphotos.com*

Good Chi, Bad Chi, and Poison Arrows

Chi can be positive or negative, good or bad. Positive chi brings health, wealth, abundant opportunities, and happy family relationships, while bad chi brings accidents, bad luck, poverty, and sometimes even illness or death. The main goal of Feng Shui is to attract and create good chi and to deflect and eliminate bad chi.

Killing chi can be caused by natural or man-made environmental factors that create *poison arrows*. These lines of destructive force can occur inside or outside a house and are caused by straight lines, sharp edges and angles, and projecting corners of roads, buildings, and furnishings (even the blades of a ceiling fan!). Large structures that dwarf your house, or menacing natural features, such as an overhanging boulder, also create bad chi. Install a yin bagua mirror (see page 16) or other reflective material over your front door to deflect bad chi.

Chi can also stagnate due to clutter or lack of natural light or go rocketing out of your house because of the wrong placement of doors, windows, or furniture. But don't worry, there are solutions for all these problems (see Quick and Easy Feng Shui Remedies, page 32).

Yin and Yang

The concept of two kinds of energy called yin and yang is fundamental to Taoism and Feng Shui. The idea that the universe is in a continual state of change, moving between yin and yang, seeking a state of balance, was first expressed in the ancient Chinese text called the *I Ching*, or Book of Changes. Yin and yang are relative terms used to compare the world around us, and every person, object, material, and process can be analyzed as more yin or yang when compared to something else. Yin is a dark, moist, soft, yielding, quiet energy, an energy of stillness and, taken to an extreme, lifelessness. Yang is a bright, dry, hard, active, lively (even noisy) energy.

Soft materials such as bamboo or wood are considered yin, while hard, shiny materials are yang. In terms of shapes, anything that has a stabilizing or grounding effect (a square, for example) is yin, while anything that could move (a sphere, for example) is yang. By following the principles of Feng Shui to balance and harmonize yin and yang energies when you furnish and decorate your home, you'll attract the chi that supports the activities you typically pursue in different areas. This is common-sense Feng Shui: a bright, sunny (yang) room keeps you alert while you work, while relaxation or meditation is easier in a shady (yin) spot.

Places to Avoid

Avoid living near areas that generate yin energy, such as cemeteries, or destructive energy, such as power stations, law enforcement facilities, or landfills and dumps. Instead, pick out areas close to forests, farms, or parks, places where children congregate, and spiritual and healing centers (*not* a traditional hospital). These all generate positive, yang energy.

The Lo Pan

Feng Shui geomancers use the *lo pan* to determine the best site for a home and the location of its architectural features by calculating interactions among trigrams, elements, and astrological influences. The face of this lo pan, designed by Master Chan Kun Wah of Edinburgh, Scotland, contains

CONTINUED ON PAGE 16

formulas and codes within dozens of concentric rings around a small compass. Laypeople who follow Compass School generally use a Western-style compass and work from tables of formulas calculated by Feng Shui masters.

Early Heaven

The trigrams on this bagua mirror are in the Early Heaven arrangement, traditionally used for the planning and placement of gravesites, which the Chinese believed to be very important in ensuring a spirit's happy repose and the passage of good luck to descendants. This mirror is considered an extremely powerful antidote to killing chi and should never be hung indoors or where it can

FIGURE 2

deflect bad chi toward a neighbor's house. Figure 2 features trigrams in the later Heaven sequence, used in homes and offices.

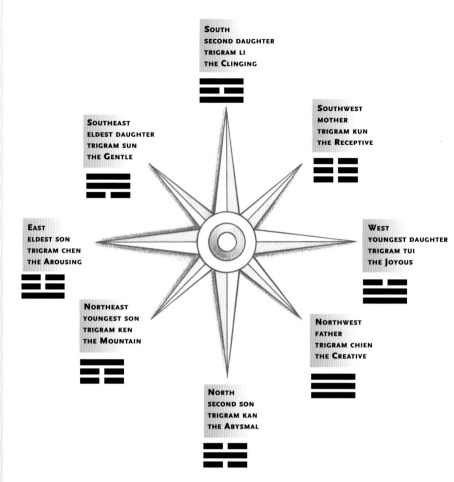

SOUTH
SECOND DAUGHTER
TRIGRAM LI
THE CLINGING

SOUTHEAST
ELDEST DAUGHTER
TRIGRAM SUN
THE GENTLE

SOUTHWEST
MOTHER
TRIGRAM KUN
THE RECEPTIVE

EAST
ELDEST SON
TRIGRAM CHEN
THE AROUSING

WEST
YOUNGEST DAUGHTER
TRIGRAM TUI
THE JOYOUS

NORTHEAST
YOUNGEST SON
TRIGRAM KEN
THE MOUNTAIN

NORTHWEST
FATHER
TRIGRAM CHIEN
THE CREATIVE

NORTH
SECOND SON
TRIGRAM KAN
THE ABYSMAL

FIGURE 1
LATER HEAVEN SEQUENCE OF TRIGRAMS

The I Ching and the Trigrams

The *I Ching* was originally based on eight different three-tiered groupings of solid and broken lines called *trigrams*. The broken lines represent yin energy, the solid lines yang energy, and the *trigrams* reflect different proportions of yin and yang. Legend says that a ruler named Fu Hsi (foo SHEE) invented the trigrams 4,500 years ago, after studying the patterns on the back of a tortoise. (A later ruler named King Wen combined the trigrams into 64 different permutations of six lines each called *hexagrams*. But it's the original eight trigrams that are of interest in Feng Shui.)

Trigrams and Points of the Compass

Read from top to bottom, the three lines of a trigram represent *tien ti ren* [tyin TEE rin], or heaven, man, and earth respectively. Each trigram is affiliated with a specific compass direction and one of the five elements, as shown in figure 1. The trigrams shown are in the Later Heaven arrangement, which is yang in nature and therefore appropriate for homes, offices, and other places of human activity.

The Five Elements

In Feng Shui, all things on earth—even colors, shapes, and numbers—are associated with one of five basic elements: Water, Wood, Earth, Fire, or Metal. In turn, each element is classified as predominantly yin or yang.

Bear in mind that the five elements have nothing to do with the table of elements taught in chemistry class. Rather they represent five fundamentally different types of energy. The elemental energy called Water flows beneath an apparently calm surface; Wood moves upward; Earth moves downward; Fire radiates outward in all directions; and Metal moves inward, much like metal ore forms under tremendous pressures deep inside the planet's core. You'll want to become very familiar with the five elements and how they interact, because the five elements are absolutely integral to Feng Shui practice.

How the Five Elements Relate to One Another

The five elements stand in dynamic relationship to one another and affect each other in specific ways as shown in the charts and illustration on pages 18 and 19. These four patterns of interaction are called the *enhancing, controlling, weakening*, and *mediating* cycles. By becoming familiar with these cycles, you'll understand how to balance the energies of a space by removing or adding elements (see How to Use the Bagua, page 24, to learn exactly *where* in a room to do *what*).

The relationships between some elements are easy to perceive, while others are more subtle. It helps to think like a poet! For example, it seems obvious that wood feeds fire and water destroys fire. But wood also destroys earth in the sense that trees sap the energies contained in the earth.

The Enhancing, Controlling, and Weakening Cycles

In the enhancing cycle, an element feeds or energizes another specific element, while in the controlling cycle, one element reduces another. Note that the controlling cycle isn't simply the reverse of the creative cycle. The weakening cycle is useful when you want to lessen a dominant element in a room without completely obliterating its influence. How much to add? Whatever looks and feels good to you. Then pay attention to any changes you experience in the atmosphere of your home.

The Mediating Cycle

The mediating cycle can be used for advanced applications of Compass School Feng Shui (when a person's birth element conflicts with the direction

---

The Five Elements

WATER

The lotus flower, which grows in water, is an ancient symbol of spiritual enlightenment and a bringer of good fortune.

WOOD

Paper, wicker, and even the rattan used to construct this tray are all activators of Wood energy.

EARTH

Like the depths of the earth from which they came, gemstones carry Earth energy.

FIRE

Flame and flame shapes activate Fire energy.

METAL

Metallic materials and finishes generate Metal energy.

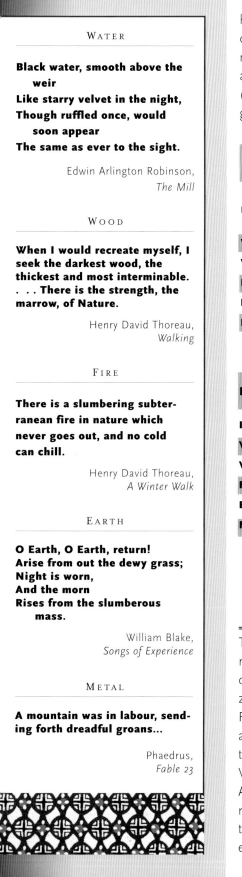
her front door faces, for example). The mediating cycle can also be used to calm a conflict between elements in the home. For example, the powerful elements of Fire and Water are frequently too close together in kitchens, creating an unsettled atmosphere (see page 36). Or perhaps you have a bathroom (Water) in the northeast (Earth) part of your home—a combination which generates mud! Use remedies from the charts below.

ENHANCING CYCLE		CONTROLLING CYCLE	WEAKENING CYCLE
ELEMENT	**ENHANCES**	**CONTROLS**	**WEAKENS**
WATER	**WOOD**	**FIRE (IF WOOD IS WEAK)**	**METAL**
WOOD	**FIRE**	**EARTH (IF FIRE IS WEAK)**	**WATER**
FIRE	**EARTH**	**METAL (IF EARTH IS WEAK)**	**WOOD**
EARTH	**METAL**	**WATER (IF METAL IS WEAK)**	**FIRE**
METAL	**WATER**	**WOOD (IF WATER IS WEAK)**	**EARTH**

MEDIATING CYCLE	
IF	**CALM WITH**
WATER CONFLICTS WITH FIRE	**WOOD**
WOOD CONFLICTS WITH EARTH	**FIRE**
FIRE CONFLICTS WITH METAL	**EARTH**
EARTH CONFLICTS WITH WATER	**METAL**
METAL CONFLICTS WITH WOOD	**WATER**

How the Five Elements Relate to Compass Directions

The sun's movement defines how the five elements and compass directions relate to one another. In the morning, the eastern part of your home is charged by upwardly moving Wood energy. As the sun moves into its midday zenith, your home's southern exposures are charged with the radiance of the Fire element. As the sun begins to lower in the southwest, the southwestern and center parts of your home will feel downward Earth energy. At sundown, the western exposure feels inwardly directed Metal energy. And at night, Water, flowing beneath stillness, energizes your home's northern exposure. Although the energies of each part of the home may decrease when they're not being actively charged, they retain their elemental nature. For example, the southern exposure of a house, or of a room, retains the character and energy of Fire even at night.

Cycle of the Five Elements

Auspicious shapes of Buildings and Interiors

Good Feng Shui calls for balance and considers certain shapes to be very auspicious: squares, rectangles, circles, and octagons. Crosses, triangles, and irregular shapes should be avoided. This applies to buildings and interiors, too. You'll therefore want to correct any major irregularities in the shape of a room, such as a projecting corner, before you begin energizing the space. See Asymmetrical Rooms (page 33) for some easy solutions.

AUSPICIOUS

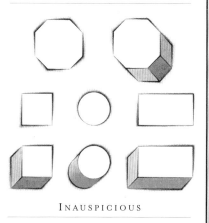

INAUSPICIOUS

IMPROVING YOUR HOME'S CHI

Before you start using the five elements to improve your home's energies, there are many adjustments you can make to balance yin and yang, block bad chi, and attract, accumulate, and circulate good chi. It's important to avoid the negative and approach the positive: Get rid of conductors of bad energy first, then work on attracting good energy.

As you learn to operate from a Feng Shui point of view, you'll think like a poet *and* act very literally. For example, to restore restful energies to a bedroom, you might add a throw rug or a carpet in a "heavy," i.e., dark color. That's the poetic part, finding aesthetic equivalents between things. Or you might calm unsettled energies in the same bedroom by installing a very heavy piece of furniture or sculpture. That's the literal part. Either way, Feng Shui operates according to the principle "Like attracts like." If an object moves or breathes, whether it's animal, plant, or wind chime, it helps circulate chi. If it hugs the ground, it "grounds" chi.

Eliminate the Negative

Banish dirt, clutter, and darkness from your life. Chi doesn't like any of them! So give your house the best spring cleaning it's ever had, no matter what time of year it is. Clean out closets, cupboards, attic, basement, and garage. Keeping only what is beautiful or useful to you, haul everything else to a local charity or have the biggest yard sale of all time. Chi can't enter places that are choked with unused or broken belongings (and you'll also want to make room for the beautiful things this book shows you how to make), so repair them or get rid of them.

Light is the most powerful generator of healthy chi, so make sure it can enter your house. Choose a home with an ample, but not overwhelming, number of windows. Pry open any stuck windows and clean them until they sparkle. Move any furniture that prevents a door from swinging completely open and shut. Hang mirrors but don't go overboard or the excess yang energy will prevent your home from feeling restful.

Dealing with Poison Arrows and Cutting Chi

Do a visual check for any poison arrows in your home, as shown in figure 1. Position furniture so no exposed ceiling beams, sharp edges, jutting corners, ceiling fan blades, or looming overhangs aim cutting or oppressive energy at the places you sit or sleep. At worst, poison arrows are said to harm one's health. At best, they still disturb the smooth flow of energy and create an unsettled, discordant atmosphere. Soften or hide poison arrows with lush trailing plants. Hang banners or position screens in front of problem areas.

Some Feng Shui enthusiasts hang bamboo flutes, wind chimes, or faceted crystals to neutralize cutting chi. Round, prismatic crystals are hung from the center of a ceiling fan to interrupt the cutting chi created by the fan blades. You might even hang them with red cord cut in lengths that are multiples of nine, an auspicious number. Or you may prefer using monofilament for a more discreet look. Make sure direct sunlight cannot hit a crystal or it may create a fire hazard.

If you use crystals, choose clear or white ones unless you're familiar with the qualities and reputed effects of different crystals. The energies of colored crystals can create more problems than they solve.

Accentuate the Positive

Now you're ready to invite auspicious Feng Shui to enter. The easiest way is to energize the element associated with each sector of the bagua, or each compass direction, as explained below. But don't go overboard. Remember the key principles of balance and harmony. In Feng Shui, too much of a good thing is simply that—too much!

To apply Feng Shui even more effectively, you need to learn how to use Feng Shui's most important tool, the *bagua*.

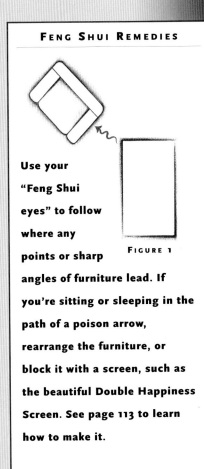

The Role of Trigrams in the Later Heaven Bagua

Remember the eight trigrams of the *I Ching*, mystically divined by Fu Hsi from the shell of a tortoise? The Chinese believe the bagua derives its power from the arrangement of the eight trigrams on the eight sides of

the bagua. In turn, the symbolism of each trigram gives meaning to its affiliated compass direction. You'll note that, unlike Western tradition, north is at the bottom. This is due to the importance of the *lo shu*, or magic square, in Compass School Feng Shui. Studying the sequence of the patterns on the tortoise shell, Fu Hsi derived a mystical sequence of numbers oriented

CONTINUED ON PAGE 23

WHAT IS THE BAGUA?

All the different mystical traditions and analytical aspects of Feng Shui come together in the *bagua*: the eight trigrams, the directions of the compass, the five elements, and their associated materials, colors, and influences.

The bagua literally maps out the energy sectors that affect family members and key aspects of their lives within a home or a room. Each gua, or sector of the bagua, always stands in the same relationship to the other sectors.

You can choose between two types of baguas to use in analyzing your home's Feng Shui. The first is the Later Heaven bagua shown on page 23. Used by Form School practitioners, it's based on a specific arrangement of trigrams and their associated compass directions, which in turn affect the fortunes of specific family members.

The second type of bagua shown on page 24 is very popular among Westerners. The bagua's nine guas correspond to nine aspects of a person's life: Wealth, Fame, Relationship, Children and Creativity, Helpful People and Travel, Life's Path, Knowledge, and Health and Family, plus the ninth gua in the middle called the Center. For the purposes of this book, we'll refer to this second bagua as the Aspects of Life bagua.

Once you choose which bagua to use, you'll also have a choice of using compass directions or the location of doorways to orient the bagua to your home. Read on for more information to help you make a choice that feels right to you.

The Forbidden City in Beijing, shown in the above photo, was the magnificent residence of Chinese emperors for thousands of years. Feng Shui principles are manifested in its elaborate architecture, landscaping, and use of water elements. Image by Jon Bower at apexphotos.com

The Later Heaven Bagua

The trigrams and the five elements play an important role in family relationships and good fortune, including health. Each trigram and compass direction is affiliated with a particular family member, and their arrangement has a powerful influence on family relationships. Fathers and youngest daughters are close, for example, because their trigrams fall next to each other. The fortunes of each family member are affected by what happens in their sector of the bagua. For example, if the head of the household is having problems, the family should examine the northwest aspect of the house to see if trees are crowding the house or if elements are weak or in conflict.

LATER HEAVEN BAGUA

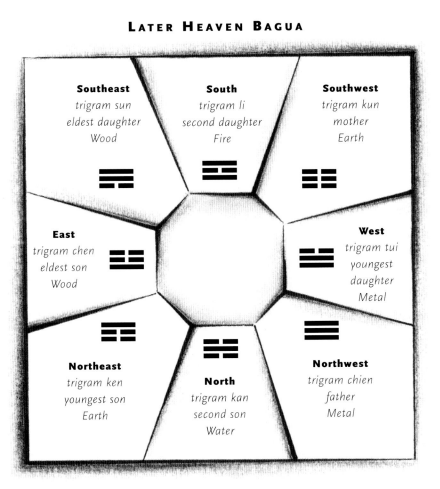

CONTINUED FROM PAGE 22

in a specific pattern within a nine-sector grid. Whether added together diagonally, vertically, or horizontally, the numbers within the magic square always total fifteen. The pattern formed by the numbers are in turn linked with the arrangement of the trigrams in the Later Heaven bagua, and the numbers correspond to specific compass points: one to the north, nine to the south, and so on, as shown below.

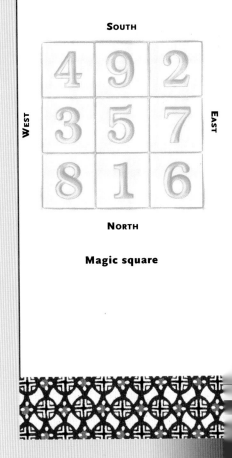

Magic square

The Later Heaven bagua is considered yang and is quite different from the Early Heaven yin bagua used to repel killing chi (see page 16). Feng Shui masters use the yin bagua when choosing the site of a home, then apply the yang bagua for room placement. Later Heaven is appropriate for areas of yang energy, populated by the living.

HOW TO CREATE A FLOOR PLAN

The bagua can be applied to individual rooms or each floor in a multilevel home. Make a simple pencil sketch of the space under consideration or, if you wish, use graph paper to draw a floor plan to scale. As shown in figure 1, be sure to lay in all exterior and interior walls, doors, windows, and staircases. Note significant fixtures such as lavatories, tubs, toilets, kitchens, and fireplaces, and any potential structural problems, such as ceiling beams, projecting corners, or sloped ceilings. Mark where you plan to position pieces of furniture, too. To find the center of a room, draw lines connecting opposing corners (fig. 2).

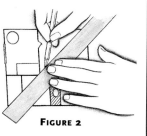

FIGURE 1

FIGURE 2

CONTINUED ON PAGE 25

The Aspects of Life Bagua

The bagua shown below is very popular among Westerners and originated with Compass School Feng Shui. Its guas represent Wealth, Fame, Relationship, Travel and Helpful People, Life's Path, Knowledge, and Health and Family, plus the ninth sector in the middle called the Center. The different energies in each gua affect different aspects of one's life.

ASPECTS OF LIFE BAGUA

Wealth
Rich, Expensive Materials
Purples, Blues, Reds, Greens

Fame
Triangles, Points, Cones, Zigzags
Reds, Maroons

Relationship
Tactile, Sensual Materials
Pinks, Reds, Yellows, Whites

Health & Family
Wood, Wicker, Bamboo, Paper
Greens, Blues

Center
Earth, Plaster, China, Brick, Tile
Yellows, Browns

Children & Creativity
Metals, Gems, Hard Stones
Gold, Silver, Whites,

Knowledge
Earth, Plaster, China, Brick, Tile
Dark Greens and Blues, Black

Life's Path
Glass, Water
Black, Blues, Dark Colors

Helpful People & Travel
Metals, Metallic Finishes
Black, White, Grays

How to Use the Bagua to Analyze Your Home

You can apply the bagua to your entire house, individual rooms, or a desktop. It's most important to adjust the Feng Shui of individual rooms—especially places where you spend a lot of time, such as a bedroom—because their elemental energies are most powerful.

To use the bagua to properly analyze the energies of a space, there are a few things you must do first: create a floor plan, choose the bagua with which you'd like to work, and orient the bagua to the floor plan.

How to Orient the Bagua to the Floor Plan

Once you've decided whether you'd like to use the Later Heaven or the Aspects of Life bagua (pages 23 and 24), make a tracing or photocopy it onto a piece of clear acetate, enlarging it as needed.

Lay the bagua over the floor plan, matching the Center gua to the central point of the floor plan. Draw extensions of the boundaries of the guas as they radiate from the center if necessary. Once you've drawn the extensions, you'll see that each wall is divided roughly into thirds and the entire space into nine sectors. Because of the bagua's shape, the corner sectors will be a little larger.

Now you're ready to orient the different sectors of the bagua to the floor plan. There are several ways to do this, depending on which bagua you're using.

ORIENTING THE LATER HEAVEN BAGUA

To orient the Later Heaven bagua to the floor plan, rotate them until their compass directions match up: north to north, south to south, and so on, as shown in figure 1.

ORIENTING THE ASPECTS OF LIFE BAGUA

There are three ways you can orient the Aspects of Life bagua to the floor plan, and the first two involve compass directions. One choice is to point the Fame sector south (fig. 2). A second school of thought recommends guarding a family's health by aligning the Health and Family sector with the west (page 26, fig. 3).

Many Westerners use a third method called the "entrance method." Find the wall that contains the main entrance to the room and align the Life's

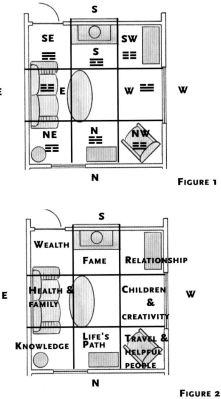

FIGURE 1

FIGURE 2

HOW TO CREATE A FLOOR PLAN, CONTINUED

Now you need to locate the center of the space. Photocopy the floor plan or draw it on tracing paper, then cut it out. Glue or tape the cutout to a piece of cardboard. To find the center of a room, draw lines connecting opposite corners.

To find the center of the entire house or an irregularly shaped space, place the cutout on top of a long straight pin, moving the cardboard around until it balances on the pinpoint (fig. 3). The center lies at the tip of the pin. If you're trying to find the center of an irregularly shaped room, glue some tissue paper in the "missing" area; the center may lie there.

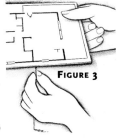

FIGURE 3

Finally, use a compass to locate the eight directions (N, NE, E, SE, S, SW, W, NW) and mark them on the plan (fig. 4).

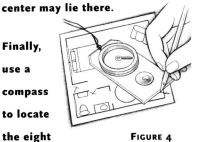

FIGURE 4

Path sector with it (fig. 4). If there's more than one door, pick the one closest to the main entrance of the house. Ignore any permanently sealed doors and pick the one most used. If you've done this correctly, the Wealth area should lie to the far left of the main entrance. If a house has more than one story, the wall you're facing when you've stepped up or down to the new level is the one to match up with the Life's Path sector.

Feng Shui recommends that you not mix the compass and entrance methods of aligning the bagua, with one exception. If you're using the entrance method and a main door stands at an angle without obviously being part of the wall on either side, you can use your intuition to choose a wall or use the compass method for that room only.

But whether you match the bagua to a room by aligning Fame to the south, Health and Family to the west, or Life's Path with the main door, the Bagua Compass Table on page 27 is a wonderful tool for quickly determining where the other sectors lie. And it makes a very attractive side table!

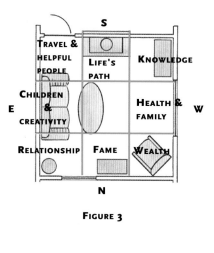

FIGURE 3

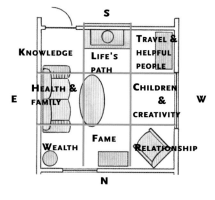

FIGURE 4

Interpreting the Bagua and Making Changes

Okay, you've aligned the bagua with the floor plan to your satisfaction. Now it's time to consult your own experience and intuition about areas of your life you'd like to enrich and improve. Whether you've decided you could use more love, more money, or more help with the kids, the Bagua Table project on the next page is both beautiful and useful, helping you locate the places in your home that could use some improved energy!

Do you also remember the Feng Shui maxim that you should fix existing problems before taking steps to energize the bagua? Chapter two (page 32) explains common Feng Shui problems found inside a home and easy solutions, including how-to projects to balance the Five Elements and energize good chi. Chapter three (page 80) details a real-life Feng Shui home makeover. And finally, chapter four, beautiful How-To Projects for All Parts of the Bagua (page 88), explains each sector of the bagua in more detail and gives easy how-to instructions for creating beautiful objects to energize chi, sector by sector.

BAGUA TABLE

THIS MAGNIFICENT TABLE IS NOT ONLY BEAUTIFULLY EMBELLISHED WITH AN INTERPRETATION OF THE BAGUA AND ITS ASSOCIATED COLORS, MATERIALS, AND SYMBOLS, IT'S A USEFUL TOOL TO HELP YOU QUICKLY ANALYZE A ROOM'S ENERGY SECTORS. AS YOU LEARNED EARLIER IN THIS CHAPTER, ONCE YOU ALIGN THE BAGUA ACCORDING TO COMPASS DIRECTION OR THE LOCATION OF THE MAIN ENTRANCE OF A INTERIOR, THE OTHER SECTORS OF THE BAGUA FALL INTO PLACE.

Designer ● Jodi Ford

TOOLS & MATERIALS

- **small, square end table**
- **ruler**
- **pencil**
- **carbon paper (optional)**
- **very fine sandpaper**
- **tack cloth**
- **primer**
- **paintbrushes, medium and fine**
- **acrylic paints in deep purple, red, soft pink, deep pink, yellow, metallic silver, light gray, dark blue or black, metallic gold, white, and light brown**
- **water-based polyurethane**
- **assorted plastic jewels or disassembled costume jewelry**
- **hot glue gun and glue sticks**
- **star-shape sequins, stick-ons, and plastic jewels**
- **round silver sequins**
- **several travel postcards**
- **white craft glue or acrylic medium**
- **fish and wave patterns on page 43**
- **stencil brush**
- **inexpensive paperback dictionary**
- **short, trimmed pieces of bamboo about 1/8 inch (3 mm) in diameter**
- **garden shears or kitchen scissors**
- **utility knife**
- **wood stain in desired color**
- **glass cut to fit top of table (optional)**
- **4 small, clear plastic bumpers (optional)**
- **small, flat compass (optional)**

INSTRUCTIONS

1 Referring to figure 1, use the ruler and pencil to draw the same diagram on the tabletop. If you wish, use a photocopier to enlarge the diagram to the same size as the tabletop. Place the carbon paper face down on the table with the photocopy on top, and trace over the photocopy to transfer the design.

2 Lightly sand the table and wipe the dust off with the tack cloth. Coat with the primer, let dry, then lightly sand again. Wipe clean.

3 Figure 1 indicates the locations of the guas and their colors. Paint each gua its specified color. Let dry, brush on a coat of polyurethane, and let dry again. The guas are now ready to be decorated with materials, symbols, and colors that evoke the spirit or element of each gua.

4 In the Wealth gua, arrange plastic jewels or bits of costume jewelry to your satisfaction. Hot glue them in place.

5 Hot glue the star-shape embellishments to the Fame gua.

6 For the Relationships gua, copy the decorative design shown in the photo at right or create your own. If you create your own design, it should be balanced and symmetrical. Trace the image on the back of the paper, lay it face up on the table, and trace it directly onto the table. Paint the pattern with red, deep pink, and yellow.

7 Use small drops of hot glue to adhere the silver sequins to the Children and Creativity gua, ovelapping them slightly to create a dense surface.

8 Make color photocopies of the postcards, reducing them by 50 percent or more. Use the white craft glue or acrylic medium to secure them to the Helpful People and Travel gua.

9 Photocopy the fish and wave patterns on page 43 to create images to fit your table's Life's Path gua. Follow steps 2 through 4 on page 59 to make stencils. Using the gold paint, apply each stencil at selected points in the Life's Path gua. Let dry, then use the small paintbrush to add black and gold outlines and details as desired.

10 Randomly tear bits of pages from the dictionary. Using the acrylic medium, adhere them to the surface of the Knowledge gua. Try to intersperse type with illustrations.

11 To decorate the Health and Family gua, choose bamboo pieces of similar sizes. Plan a basic design and use the shears or scissors to trim the bamboo sections and the knife to split them if necessary. (Be careful. Split bamboo is very sharp!) For a clean fit where bamboo pieces meet each other or the sides of the gua at an angle, trim the ends of the bamboo to 45° angles, then hot glue them in place.

12 Give the tabletop several coats of the polyurethane. Let dry.

13 Lightly sand the unembellished parts of the table with strokes that follow the grain. Wipe clean. Brush on the stain. Let dry, lightly sand again, then apply several coats of polyurethane.

14 If you wish to cover the table with glass, fix the rubber bumpers to the four corners of the table, and lay the glass on top. If you're using a compass, position the compass in the center on top of the glass or use a little glue to adhere it directly to the wood.

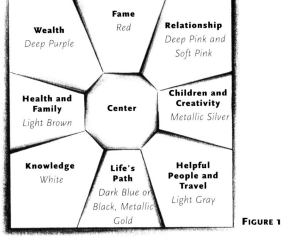

FIGURE 1

	Fame	
	Red	
Wealth		Relationship
Deep Purple		Deep Pink and Soft Pink
Health and Family	Center	Children and Creativity
Light Brown		Metallic Silver
Knowledge	Life's Path	Helpful People and Travel
White	Dark Blue or Black, Metallic Gold	Light Gray

How to Locate the Celestial Creatures and Balance the Energies Around Your Home

Form School Feng Shui analyzes the topography of the landscape surrounding a home (or potential homesite) to determine if the energies represented by the Celestial Creatures are in alignment. The focus of this book is on harmonizing Feng Shui inside your home, but there are some simple things you can do to balance the energies outside, too. Many Feng Shui masters recommend fixing any major problems outside a house before working on the inside. But if that's not practical, whatever Feng Shui improvements you make, even if they're not huge changes, could reap benefits. How to tell? Try making some changes, then be attentive to any changes in the quality of your life.

To locate the energies of the Celestial Creatures in the landscape around your house, stand inside your front door, looking out. The symbolic energies represented by Green Dragon are on your left and White Tiger on the right. Ideally, Green Dragon should be slightly elevated, i.e., stronger, than White Tiger. Why? Green Dragon represents the fortunes of the main breadwinner of the family and it also symbolizes helpful people. The property on either side of a house should also protect and cradle the dwelling, much like a pair of sheltering arms that "hug" the house. If either side of the property is much higher or more dominant than the other, landscape the property to place a light, statue, or garden feature on the lower side to symbolically restore the ideal balance of energies.

If the yard in front of your house (where the front door is) slopes gently down and the backyard slopes up, the Phoenix and Tortoise are properly aligned. The front yard, which slopes down, should be open and uncluttered so the Phoenix can "take flight" and bring prosperity. But if the front door of your home faces an up slope (true for many hillside homes), some Feng Shui practitioners recommend installing an uplight or a rooftop object such as a windcatcher on the back (lower) side of the house to direct the eye (and therefore chi) upward.

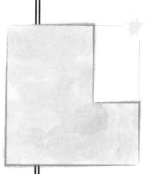

A word of caution: Fountains near the front door are very popular in the West. Water is a very powerful element, however, and can be very destructive if used improperly. If you don't absolutely need Water, don't add it without consulting a Feng Shui expert first. If you decide to go ahead and install a water feature, monitor what happens in your life afterwards. If you start to experience problems, you can always make changes.

If your home is irregular in shape, analyze which corners are "missing." Install a tall light or attention-getting statue at that corner to symbolically "complete" the shape of your house.

Using the Five Elements for Good Feng Shui: A Simple Guide

These handy charts can serve as quick references for how to use the Five Elements to enhance life for you and your family. Whether you use the Aspects of Life Bagua (page 24) or Later Heaven Bagua (page 23), each sector of the bagua is characterized by the energies of one of the Five Elements: Water, Earth, Wood, Fire, or Metal. If you experience problems in the part of your life influenced by a particular sector of the bagua, here are three possible remedies:

1 Add more of the element associated with the sector. For example, if you have problems with Life's Path, add more Water element in the form of water objects, materials, or symbols. See chapter 2 (page 32) and chapter 4 (page 88).

2 Add a second element that enhances the element associated with the sector.

3 Analyze whether the sector contains too much of an element that conflicts with the sector's associated element, and add a third element that calms the conflict.

In Feng Shui, small changes can make a big impact, so don't go overboard when adding elements or you may create new problems. For a more complete explanation of how the Five Elements interact, see pages 17 through 19.

ASPECTS OF LIFE BAGUA

BAGUA SECTOR	PROBLEM	REMEDIES
■ Life's Path—WATER	■ Are you uncertain about your goals or purpose? Are you changing careers or having a midlife crisis?	■ Increase Water element. Add Metal to enhance Water. Investigate whether there's too much Earth element in the sector. If so, add Wood.
■ Knowledge—EARTH	■ Do you seek spiritual wisdom, sharpened intuition, or a deeper knowledge of your inner self?	■ Increase Earth element. Add Fire to enhance Earth. Investigate whether there's too much Wood element in the sector. If so, add Metal.
■ Health & Family—WOOD	■ Do you or your family suffer from a continual stream of illnesses, accidents, and conflict? Would you like a greater sense of connection with your ancestors and community?	■ Increase Wood element. Add Water to enhance Wood. Investigate whether there's too much Metal element in the sector. If so, add Fire.
■ Wealth—WOOD	■ Are you continually short of money? Do resources seem to slip through your hands? Are the good things of life passing you by?	■ Increase Wood element. Add Water to enhance Wood. Investigate whether there's too much Metal element in the sector. If so, add Fire.
■ Fame—FIRE	■ Do your contributions at work or home go unnoticed? Have you failed to get the rewards and recognition you merit?	■ Increase Fire element. Add Wood to enhance Fire. Investigate whether there's too much Water element in the sector. If so, add Earth.
■ Relationship —EARTH	■ Are you lonely? Are you experiencing problems with your romantic partner, or are you having trouble finding a special someone?	■ Increase Earth element. Add Fire to enhance Earth. Investigate whether there's too much Wood element in the sector. If so, add Metal.
■ Children & Creativity — METAL	■ Are your children driving your crazy? Do you feel blocked in your expression of your mental "children," your intellectual or artistic ideas? Would you like to regain the sense of joy so natural to children?	■ Increase Metal element. Add Earth to enhance Metal. Investigate whether there's too much Fire element in the sector. If so, add Water.
■ Travel & Helpful People — METAL	■ Could you use the help of powerful friends or beneficent beings to achieve your goals and dreams? Do you feel trapped by circumstances? Do you dream of seeing the world or expanding your horizons?	■ Increase Metal element. Add Earth to enhance Metal. Investigate whether there's too much Fire element in the sector. If so, add Water.
■ Center—EARTH	■ Does your life feel fragmented and unstable? Do you seek a greater sense of security and completion?	■ Increase Earth element. Add Fire to enhance Earth. Investigate whether there's too much Wood element in the sector. If so, add Metal.

LATER HEAVEN BAGUA

The Later Heaven Bagua emphasizes the influence of the trigrams and compass directions on family relationships. Arranged by compass direction, here are the associated elements, the affiliated family member who may be experiencing problems, and some elemental remedies to try.

COMPASS DIRECTION	FAMILY MEMBER EXPERIENCING PROBLEMS	REMEDIES
South —FIRE	second daughter	Increase Fire. Add Wood.
Southwest —EARTH	mother	Increase Earth. Add Fire.
West —METAL	youngest daughter	Increase Metal. Add Earth.
Northwest —METAL	father	Increase Metal. Add Earth.
North —WATER	second son	Increase Water. Add Metal.
Northeast —EARTH	youngest son	Increase Earth. Add Fire.
East —WOOD	eldest son	Increase Wood. Add Water.
Southeast —WOOD	eldest daughter	Increase Wood. Add Water.

EASY PROJECTS TO ENERGIZE THE ELEMENTS

Starting on page 39, this chapter contains super-easy projects for energizing the Five Elements and how-to instructions for making beautiful and useful objects to attract and correct chi. They include:

Light and Life: Quick and Easy Feng Shui Remedies

When you look at your home with "Feng Shui eyes," step back and take in the larger picture. In your mind's eye, try to imagine the movement of chi as it flows through the main entrance into your home, meanders up and down halls and stairways, and gently pools in different rooms. In addition to the specific steps you can take to energize or calm chi in the different sectors of a room, there are also larger structural or lifestyle Feng Shui problems to avoid or correct. Once you've dealt with those problems, proceed to Now for the Fun Part (page 37) for simple ways to attract chi.

You'll be amazed to learn how many architectural features commonly found in Western homes are actually problematic or downright disastrous from the Feng Shui point of view. Read on to learn about the most common ones (and how to fix them).

The spacious feeling and earth tones of this living room perfectly support the energies of its position in the Center of the home.

Long, Straight Lines

Chi will pick up speed and barrel through a hallway like the one shown in the photo at lower right, or down long, straight paths formed by architectural features or furniture, giving your home an unsettled feeling. Install lights, hang art on the walls, and stagger furniture, plants, or statuary to attract chi's attention and get it to slow down and meander through.

Doors in a Line

If any room has two doors that both lead to the outdoors and which are also directly opposite each other, chi will blow into your house and straight out again. Three doors in a line are even worse! Position a screen in between two of the doors, as shown in figure 1, and use the same remedies for long, straight hallways to get chi to slow down and stay awhile.

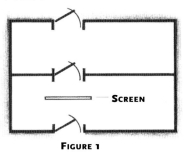

— **SCREEN**

FIGURE 1

Cutting Corners

Any corner that forms a sharp edge, which in turn juts into a room, can create cutting chi, which affects everyone in its path. Hang a wind chime, curtain, or banner over the edge, or position a tall potted plant or a gracefully dangling plant so the leaves soften the corner (see Corner Plant Shelf, page 60). Some Feng Shui practitioners hang hollow bamboo stems or flutes tied with red thread to symbolically transform damaging chi as it passes through the bamboo to emerge as good energy.

Stagnant Corners

Analyze the condition of the corners of each room. If they are dim, silent, or dusty, chi will stagnate there, too. Add some yang energizers and chi attractants.

Asymmetrical Rooms

An oddly shaped room suffers from poison arrows created by protruding corners, and its asymmetry lacks the balance that Feng Shui counsels. Hang a mirror (the larger, the better) on the wall. The mirror "moves back" the wall, creating more apparent depth and restoring symmetry to the room by making it closer in appearance to a square or rectangle. Use a pristine, new mirror if you can, and be aware of the scene or object it reflects because the reflection doubles that object's energetic power.

PROJECTS TO ATTRACT & CORRECT CHI

FENG SHUI REMEDIES

If you have artwork of horses in your home, make sure they're not positioned as if they're running out your front door, or chi will run out too!

CONTINUED ON PAGE 35

Exposed Ceiling Beams and Overhangs

Exposed beams and overhangs, especially those with sharp edges, create cutting chi and a feeling of pressure. Feng Shui considers them a very serious problem if they're positioned above an area where you spend a lot of time. If you can't afford to cover the beams with a dropped ceiling, there are other structural options: one substantial and one simple. Build columns that run from the floor up to the ceiling or to be more precise, the bottoms of the beams. Or install wooden molding on both ends of each beam in the angle formed by the underside of the beam and the wall. If that's not a realistic solution for you, paint the the beams the same color as the ceiling and drape them with creeping plants. Or add fabric panels draped to form mini-canopies that hide the beams.

Some Feng Shui practitioners hang wind chimes or crystals from the beams, or they affix a pair of hollow bamboo stems or flutes at a 45° angle on the overhang, the mouthpieces of the flutes down and toward the walls.

Sloping Ceilings

Sloping ceilings compress chi, creating an intense atmosphere as opposed to a restful one. One dramatic solution would be to paint the ceiling to look like the sky, complete with clouds or stars. To encourage chi to move upward, some Feng Shui practitioners also install tall plants and up-lights or torchère lamps. The bedroom shown in the photo below was also painted a deep green around its perimeter to increase the contrast with the ceiling and "lift" the eye. If you have sloped ceilings in a bedroom, some Feng Shui practitioners recommend not using plants as a remedy because of their lively yang energy. Let your feelings be your guide!

Ceiling Fans

The most effective remedy is to reposition a bed (or sofa, chair, or dining table) so it doesn't lie underneath the cutting energy of fan blades. Paint the fan blades to match the ceiling. Some practitioners also hang spherical, faceted crystals from the centers of fans to interrupt the cutting chi.

Glass Walls, Glass Doors, and Problem Window Coverings

If you have any large glass walls or sliding glass doors, the best remedy is to cover them with a screen or, at the very least, draperies or semi-opaque sheers to keep chi from leaking out. If your windows feature venetian blinds or vertical blinds, adjust their angles so they don't aim cutting chi at you.

Fireplaces

If a fireplace dominates the center of the house, lies in the Health and Family sector of the bagua, or is visible when you walk in the front door, block the view of the fireplace if you can and calm its Fire element to keep it from burning up good chi! Remove Metal element objects and add Earth or Water element.

Furniture

Avoid interior decorating motifs or furniture with points, sharp angles, or edges that can create poison arrows and cutting chi. Ditto for open shelves and glass tables. You may, however, use round or oval-shape tables with edges that have also been rounded. You can also place a large object between you and the poison arrow or soften it with a plant,

NEGATIVE   **POSITIVE**

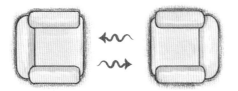

fabric drape, or tablecloth. Avoid locating pieces of furniture, such as chairs, "in confrontation," facing each other head on.

Accessories and Decorations

Given that symbolism is so important in Feng Shui, it's inadvisable to collect art that represents ruins, body parts, conflict, or fierce animals. Get rid of objects and images associated with unhappy or failed relationships, too, so there's room for good chi to enter!

CONTINUED FROM PAGE 34

The green walls and ceramic platter above the stove add Earth element to calm the Fire of this kitchen. The mirror behind the storage canisters "doubles" the food they contain and their associated prosperity luck.

Like other plants with heart-shaped or round leaves, the succulent called jade plant (*Crassula ovata*) generates prosperity luck when placed in a Wood element location, and its rounded leaves are good for blocking cutting chi. It's also known as the wealth plant because its leaves resemble pieces of the valuable gemstone.

THAT SINKING FEELING: MORE BATHROOM TIPS

Bathrooms can create real Feng Shui problems. Because chi acts like water and literally escapes through open drains, keep sinks and tubs stoppered or covered with a strainer. Keep toilet covers down (*especially* during flushing!) and bathroom doors closed. Some practitioners also position substantial rocks underneath the toilet tank and attach a small, round mirror to the ceiling directly above the center of the toilet to deflect unhealthy chi back to the source.

Windowless bathrooms need a major injection of yang energy. See page 85 for a classic Feng Shui bathroom makeover. If your home has a worst-case bathroom because it's located in the very center of your home and will therefore act like a giant drain sucking away chi, either move to a new house (!) or install mirror panels on all of the bathroom walls, ceiling, and door to seal in bad energies.

Fire and Water: Problem Bathrooms, Kitchens, and Appliances

Homeowners are usually stuck with someone else's decisions about the placement of bathrooms, kitchens, and major appliances. But you should do your best to harmoniously balance Water and Fire in those areas because they're present in their purest forms and their conflict unsettles the energy of the whole house. Think of what happens, for example, when you put a spoon of cold water into a red-hot skillet. Now think of what happens when you put a spoon of *hot* water into the same skillet. Just as Chinese medicine seeks to weaken the elements that contribute to an illness rather than obliterate a patient's symptoms, so Feng Shui approaches elemental conflicts.

Fire rules the kitchen and can be calmed with Earth. If a kitchen's Water objects (sink, dishwasher, refrigerator) are next to Fire objects (stove, microwave, toaster), separate them with Metal: a container or a metal bulletin board attached to the side of the refrigerator. Add a potted plant or something green because Wood weakens Water. Put away any cutting implements, too.

Water dominates bathrooms and should be calmed with Wood or a stronger antagonist, Earth. If a bathroom opens directly into the kitchen, always keep the door closed and install a mirror on the outside of the door. And if by some chance a toilet lies on the opposite side of a wall it shares in common with the stove in an adjoining kitchen, attach a mirror to the wall behind the stove, the mirrored side against the wall, to block the conflict of Fire and Water. If you apply the bagua to an entire floor of your home, you may see that the kitchen Fire or bathroom Water element conflicts with the guas in which the rooms lie. For example, a kitchen may lie in the Life's Path gua, which is Water element. Refer to the Mediating Cycle (page 18) for remedies.

Now for the Fun Part:
How to Attract Chi

Once you've corrected problems, add things that chi loves: light, life, movement, color, and sound! Remember that, as far as chi is concerned, appearance counts the same as reality. For example, you can invite wealth into your home with a dish of chocolate "coins" covered in gold foil rather than genuine gold bullion. In the same way, a surface marbleized with paint can add yang energies like the real (and much more expensive) material.

Some Feng Shui practitioners recommend hanging prismatic crystals at the midpoints of windows. Position wind chimes and lights to energize dark corners because chi loves light and life. Adopt cats or dogs from the local shelter. They add living yang energy to your home, as does a fish tank (which happens to be a powerful wealth attractor, too). Keep a radio or CD player on because music and sound create good chi.

The color red is extremely popular among western practitioners of Feng Shui. Using any shade of red in the western aspect of a room is auspicious, but you can also add more light and other bright colors to activate chi in the other directions. (Some Feng Shui masters believe too much red has a bad effect on health and family relations.) So if you like red, go ahead and use it. If you experience any negative results, you can always repaint. And if you've already painted your front door red, no problem! Simply paint the top and bottom white to change its trigram from Fire to Water.

Plants are wonderful for balancing a home's energies. Round leaves create a calmer, more yin chi while pointed or spiky leaves increase yang energy. Some Feng Shui practitioners think silk plants are just as good as living plants, but regardless of your preferences

CONTINUED ON PAGE 38

Encourage abundance and prosperity by displaying images of food in your kitchen or dining area. Better yet, keep a basket or tray brimming with real fruit nearby. Or try "doubling" your prosperity luck by positioning mirrors near places you prepare and serve food.

If you can wield scissors, you can make the Abundance Fruit Baskets project on page 127.

See page 97 to learn how easy it is to make this beautiful Glass Tabletop Fountain.

in that area, always avoid dried, i.e., dead plants. Anything that creates, catches, and refracts light is also good (though don't go overboard). Use lamps, mirrors, wind chimes, and/or prismatic crystals.

Indoor fountains also attract chi, but use them carefully or they may do more harm than good. Utilize the bagua (pages 23 and 24) and the Elemental Cycles (page 17) to analyze the effect of increasing the Water element in a particular sector. For example, you don't want to wash away well-being by adding too much Water element in the Life's Path sector. If in doubt, get expert advice.

Dragon imagery, such as the embellishment on this antique Chinese pot, helps wake up the yang energies of a room.

More Solutions

Have you identified some problems in your home? Are you also ready to make some beautiful objects to balance your home's energies and to attract good chi? Review the chart on page 31 to help you identify the right elements and objects to use. Here are super-fast instructions for creating and modifying basic home decorating items—trays, pillows, picture frames, and vessels—to energize the five elements. If you want to attract good chi or block poison arrows, you'll find how-to solutions here, too.

EASY FENG SHUI TRAYS

IN EARTH, FIRE, & WATER

WOULD YOU LIKE TO ADD EARTH POWER TO YOUR RELATIONSHIPS USING THE TRAY SHOWN BELOW, OR WATER TO HELP YOU FIND YOUR LIFE'S PATH? REVIEW THE CHART ON PAGE 31, THEN PICK AMONG THE COLORS AND SYMBOLS ASSOCIATED WITH EACH ELEMENT TO DECORATE READY-MADE TRAYS. WHEN YOU PAINT THEM, APPLY MULTIPLE COATS OF PAINT AND LET THEM DRY BETWEEN COATS TO ACHIEVE A RICH, LACQUERLIKE FINISH.

Designer ● Terry Taylor

TOOLS & MATERIALS

- **unfinished wooden tray***
- **acrylic gloss paint, light green**
- **paintbrush**
- **assorted decorative papers in creams, greens, and browns**
- **pattern below**
- **scissors**
- **craft glue**
- **sheet of single-pane glass****

*Sold at craft stores

**Have the glass cut to fit the tray at your local glass shop or home improvement store.

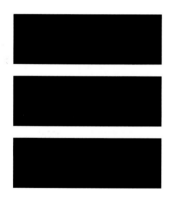

FIGURE 1

INSTRUCTIONS

1 Paint the tray green. Let dry.

2 Cut or tear the paper to fit inside the tray, leaving a border between paper and inside edge of tray. Glue in place. Cut small rectangles from a contrasting paper and arrange them to form trigrams made of three solid bars (figure 1). This is the Chien trigram, symbolizing heaven. Glue in place.

3 Lay the glass inside the tray.

FIRE TRAY

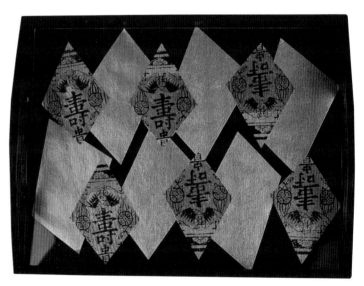

INSTRUCTIONS

1 Paint the tray red. Let dry.

2 Cut the decorative papers into pointed and triangular shapes to symbolize Fire element. Arrange them as desired, then glue in place.

3 Lay the glass inside the tray.

WATER TRAY

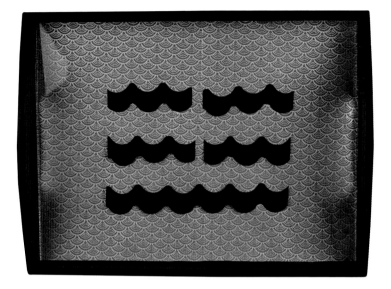

INSTRUCTIONS

1 Paint the tray dark blue. Let dry.

2 Use the decorative scissors to cut the wave-patterned paper to fit inside the tray. Glue in place.

3 Trace or photocopy the wave pattern, and cut out multiples from the black paper. Arrange as desired and glue in place.

4 Lay the glass inside the tray.

FIRE TRAY

TOOLS & MATERIALS

- acrylic gloss paint, red
- joss paper or other decorative papers in reds, golds, and oranges
- other tools and materials listed for Earth Tray on page 40

WATER TRAY

TOOLS & MATERIALS

- acrylic gloss paint, dark blue
- black paper and Japanese or other decorative paper with a stylized blue and white wave pattern
- scissors with decorative edge✻
- pattern shown
- pencil and tracing paper (optional)
- other tools and materials listed for Earth Tray on page 40

✻ Available at craft stores

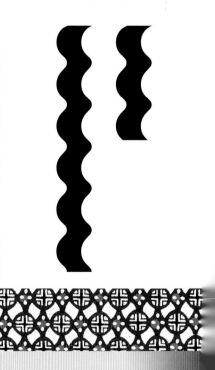

EASY FENG SHUI PILLOWS

IN WATER, WOOD, & METAL

WHAT TO DO IF YOU WANT TO ENERGIZE MORE OF A PARTICULAR ELEMENT, BUT THE FUNCTION OF THAT PART OF A ROOM DOESN'T SEEM TO AGREE? FOR EXAMPLE, WHAT IF THE BAGUA TELLS YOU THAT YOU NEED METAL OR WOOD AT THE PLACE THAT A SOFT, CUSHY SOFA SITS? THESE INVENTIVE PILLOWS HELP SOLVE THE PROBLEM BY USING COLORS, TEXTURES, AND MATERIALS THAT EMBODY PARTICULAR ELEMENTS.

Designer ● Jodi Ford

WATER PILLOW

INSTRUCTIONS

1 Measure the form, as shown in figure 1, and buy double that amount, adding 1 inch (2.5 cm) to the length and 1 inch (2.5 cm) to the width to allow for ¹/₂-inch (1.3 cm) seam allowances. If you'd like to have a self-fabric border around the pillow, add another 2 inches (5 cm) to the length and width.

2 Trim the material to two pieces in the dimensions required.

3 Photocopy the patterns at lower right, enlarging as desired to fit the pillow. Position the stencil material over the patterns, taping in place. Use the marker to trace the patterns, then carefully cut them out using the craft knife.

4 Tape or pin the piece of fabric that will serve as the pillow front to a flat surface. Mix a little of the clear fabric paint with the gold paint to thin it. Position the goldfish stencil in the center, and use the stencil brush to lightly "punch" the gold paint through the stencil. Let dry. Repeat the procedure to apply the wave stencil. Let dry. Follow the manufacturer's instructions to set the fabric paint.

5 Pin the two pieces of fabric right sides together. Use a ¹/₂-inch (1.3 cm) seam to stitch three sides together. Remove the pins. If you're not a sewer, use the fusible

tape and iron the three sides closed. (Note: If you leave the seam at the bottom of the pillow open, it's a good way to disguise the handwork needed to close the opening.)

6 Turn the pillow cover right side out. If you allowed for a fabric "border," repin the sides so they won't shift, and stitch a 1-inch (2.5 cm) seam around the perimeter of the pillow.

7 Stuff the form inside. Hand-stitch the fourth side closed, turning in the raw edges. To complete the "border," press down on the foam as you make a straight seam 1 inch (2.5 cm) from the edge of the pillow.

8 Hand-sew a tassel to each corner of the pillow.

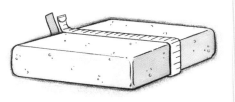

FIGURE 1

TOOLS & MATERIALS

- foam pillow form
- tape measure
- fabric in a deep, rich dark green or blue
- scissors
- patterns below
- blank stencil sheets
- masking tape
- black fine-tip permanent marker
- craft knife
- straight pins (optional)
- fabric paint in gold and in "clear"
- small dish or palette
- stencil brush
- iron
- sewing machine (optional)
- fusible tape (optional)
- sewing thread in blue and gold to match the fabric and tassels
- 4 gold tassels
- sewing needle
- ✻ See step 1 for how to calculate the amount of fabric needed to cover the pillow you select.

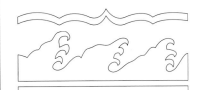

TOOLS & MATERIALS

- **fabric in a metallic color with a shiny finish, such as rayon taffeta, chintz, or lamé**
- **foam pillow form**
- **large button with metallic finish**
- **sewing thread to match the fabric**
- **metallic fringe, in a length equal to circumference of pillow plus ¹⁄₂ inch (1.3 cm)**
- **other tools and materials listed for Water Pillow on page 43**
- **hot glue gun and glue sticks**

METAL PILLOW

INSTRUCTIONS

1 Follow steps 1 through 2 and 5 through 7 of the Water Pillow to construct the pillow cover.

2 To embellish the pillow, hand-stitch the button to the center of the pillow and stitch or hot glue the fringe to the edges of the pillow, turning under ¹⁄₄ inch (6 mm) at each raw end of the fringe.

WOOD PILLOW

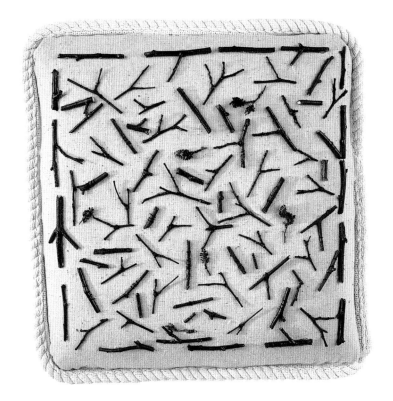

WOOD PILLOW
TOOLS & MATERIALS

- **several dozen tiny twigs cut to a variety of sizes**
- **acrylic craft paints in deep brown and dark blue**
- **waxed paper**
- **polyurethane**
- **paintbrush**
- **fabric in natural tones of cream or brown with a nubby, earthy finish**
- **foam pillow form**
- **sewing thread in a matching color**
- **other sewing tools and materials listed for Water Pillow on page 43**
- **hot glue gun and glue sticks**
- **sewing thread in a dark color**
- **cording in a matching or contrasting color, in a length equal to circumference of pillow plus ½ inch (1.3 cm)**

INSTRUCTIONS

1 Paint the twigs deep brown, adding a few dark blue highlights. Lay them on a sheet of the waxed paper and let dry, then brush lightly with polyurethane. Let dry.

2 Follow steps 1, 2, 5, and 6 of the Water Pillow on page 43. Lay the pillow cover face up on a flat surface, and arrange the twigs on top in a pattern of your choosing.

3 Lightly hot glue the twigs to the fabric, then use the dark thread to hand-stitch them in place. It's best to have three sides of the pillow already sewn together before you adhere the twigs.

4 Follow step 7 of the Water Pillow on page 43 to stuff and close the pillow.

5 Hot glue the cording to the perimeter of the pillow, turning under the raw ends.

Easy Feng Shui Frames

IN METAL, FIRE, & EARTH

It's very easy to embellish inexpensive picture frames purchased at a discount store to highlight one of the Five Elements. The embossed designs on the Metal Frame also include the ideogram for Metal and other easy-to-copy Oriental motifs.

Designer ● Jodi Ford

METAL FRAME

INSTRUCTIONS

1 Remove the backing and glass from the frame and set them aside. Lay the frame face down on the metal sheet, and use the pen or another tool to mark the edge of the frame and a border of metal around the frame. Allow for an ample margin of metal sheet to cover the frame's front and sides and overlap to the back of the frame. Mark the metal sheet that falls inside the frame in the same way, allowing enough metal to wrap inside the portrait opening. Cut away any excess metal.

2 Photocopy the patterns, reducing or enlarging as needed. If you wish to use the Metal ideogram, it must first be copied "in reverse" so it will read correctly when embossed onto the metal. To achieve this, put the photocopy of the ideogram face down against a window, lay the tracing paper on top, and make a pencil tracing.

3 Turn the metal sheet face down on the magazine, lay a pattern on top in its desired location, and use the pen or other tool to impress the pattern into the metal. Small, repetitive strokes of the tool are best.

4 When you've embossed the metal to your satisfaction, apply glue to the wrong side of the metal,

then wrap it around the frame. If the frame is circular, score the metal every few inches to insure a tight fit. Let dry.

5 To give the frame an aged look, rub the black paint over the metal and into the crevices of the embossing, then use the paper towel to wipe away the excess. Let dry. Insert the glass, a photo of your choice, and backing.

Ideogram for metal

TOOLS & MATERIALS

- **picture frame**
- **acrylic craft paints in vibrant red and black**
- **paintbrushes, medium and fine tips**
- **acrylic medium**
- **gold leaf flakes**
- **soft bristled brush**
- **adhesive metallic gold decals with zigzag edges***
- **solar pattern at right (optional)**
- **gold paper (optional)**
- **craft knife (optional)**
- **craft glue (optional)**
- **polyurethane**
- ***Office supply stores stock these seals, which are used for deeds, certificates, and awards.**

TOOLS & MATERIALS

- **picture frame**
- **acrylic craft paint in a rich, deep green**
- **small pebbles or iridescent glass beads, about ½-inch (1.3 cm) in diameter***
- **hot glue gun and glue sticks**
- ***Sold by the bag in craft stores**

FIRE FRAME

INSTRUCTIONS

1 Remove the backing and glass from the frame and paint it red. Let dry.

2 Brush the acrylic medium onto the frame. While still wet, use your fingertip to dab on the gold leaf flakes. Let dry, then use the soft bristled brush to burnish the frame, removing excess flakes.

3 Adhere the sunburst decals to the frame. Using the fine-tipped paintbrush and black paint, add black accents to the sunbursts. Let dry. Or, photocopy the solar pattern below. Trace it onto the gold paper and use the craft knife to cut out as many patterns as desired. Glue them to the frame and add the black accents.

4 Brush on a coat of the polyurethane and let dry. Insert the glass, a photo of your choice, and backing.

EARTH FRAME

INSTRUCTIONS

1 Paint the frame green and let dry.

2 Hot glue the glass beads to the front of the frame and along the edges, stacking the beads on top of each other and using enough beads so their organic shapes mask the straight edges of the frame. More is better! Insert the glass, a photo of your choice, and the backing.

EASY FENG SHUI VESSELS

IN FIRE, WATER, & EARTH

You don't need a potter's wheel or kiln to make these lovely containers. You'll use self-hardening clay and "pinch pot" construction instead. The Fire Pot has pyramidal sides, flamelike tips, and a fiery finish. The other vessels embody their elemental energies.

Designer ● Jodi Ford

FIRE POT

TOOLS & MATERIALS

- **1 to 1½ pounds (0.5 to 0.7 kg) self-hardening clay**✻
- **table knife**
- **dish of water**
- **spritzer bottle filled with water**
- **craft knife**
- **acrylic craft paint in a vibrant red**
- **paintbrush**
- **acrylic medium**
- **gold leaf flakes**
- **soft bristled brush**
- **polyurethane**
- **florist's bud tube (optional)**

✻Available at craft stores in packages of varying amounts

FIRE POT
INSTRUCTIONS

1 Divide and roll the clay into five equal, square-shaped slabs.

2 Slip and score all four edges of one slab, which will serve as the base or bottom. To slip and score, make short strokes into the surface of the clay with the knife, rub water onto the marks, then repeat the scratching-and-scoring process. This ensures a stronger join than is obtained by simply pressing moist clay edges together.

3 Take another slab and slip and score the edge that will connect to the base. Adhere it to the base, smoothing over the seam. Do this with the remaining three slabs, adhering their bottom edges to the other sides of the base slab.

4 Bring the walls of the slabs together, forming a pyramid. Smooth over the seams. Use the spritzer bottle, if necessary, to keep the clay moist so you don't have slip and score each edge before joining it to the edge of another slab.

5 Pinch the tops of the slabs so they form flamelike points. While the clay is still slightly moist and not completly dry (usually after being exposed to air for 24 hours), use the craft knife to define the flame shapes more clearly.

6 After the clay has completely hardened (as it dries, it lightens in color), paint the pot red. Let dry.

7 Apply the acrylic medium to the pot. While the medium is still wet, use your fingertips to lightly tap or dab the gold leaf flakes onto the pot. Let dry, then use the soft bristle brush to burnish the pot, removing excess gold flakes. Brush on a coat of the polyurethane for protection.

8 Because the clay is not water-safe, if you'd like to display a flower in the pot, slip the flower stem into a florist's bud tube filled with a tiny amount of water, then slip the tube into the vessel.

WATER VESSEL

INSTRUCTIONS

the tops, use the sixth slab to create a cover.

1 Follow steps 1 through 4 of the Fire Pot, but this time create six slabs and instead of forming the sides into a pyramid and pinching

2 While the clay is still wet, push the mirror tiles into the surface, being careful not to push too hard and break through the surface.

3 After the clay has hardened overnight, use your fingernail to carefully pop out the mirror tiles, then hot glue them back in place.

4 When the clay has completely hardened, paint the surface around the tiles with the black acrylic paint.

WATER VESSEL

TOOLS & MATERIALS

- **1 to 1½ pounds (0.5 to 0.7 kg) self-hardening clay**
- **48 small, square mirror tiles***
- **hot glue gun and glue sticks**
- **acrylic paint in glossy black**
- **paintbrush**

*The vessel shown used 12 tiles per side. The quantity will vary with the dimensions of your vessel.

EARTH VESSEL

INSTRUCTIONS

1 Place the plastic wrap inside the bowl, making sure there are few, if any, wrinkles in the wrap.

2 Mold the clay into the bowl so that it takes on its shape, using your fingers to smooth it out. Maintain a consistent wall thickness of about ⅛ to ¼ inch (3 to 6 mm). Use the spoon to push and prod the clay into any hard-to-reach areas and to manipulate the clay along the inner rim of the bowl so that it forms a ledge around the perimeter of the bowl.

3 Let the clay dry for 24 hours, then use the spoon to smooth away any rough spots. Extract the vessel from the bowl and peel off the plastic wrap. Let dry completely.

4 Paint the vessel and let dry. Add a coat of polyurethane and let dry. Fill with decorative pebbles or rocks if desired.

EARTH VESSEL

TOOLS & MATERIALS

- **plastic wrap**
- **small, shallow bowl to serve as the mold for the vessel**
- **1 to 1½ pounds (0.5 to 0.7 kg) self-hardening clay**
- **wooden spoon with long handle**
- **acrylic paint in hues of brown, copper, and gold**
- **paintbrush**
- **polyurethane**
- **decorative pebbles or river rocks (optional)**

BAGUA SUN CATCHER

IF YOU CAN USE A RULER TO DRAW A STRAIGHT LINE, YOU CAN MAKE THIS BEAUTIFUL FAUX STAINED GLASS BAGUA. HANG IT WHEREVER YOU THINK THE ENERGY OF A ROOM COULD USE A SHOT IN THE ARM—OR WHERE ITS RICH COLORS WILL BRING JOY TO YOUR HEART. THE SUN CATCHER SHOWN IN THE PHOTOGRAPH IS 17 INCHES (43.2 CM) ACROSS, BUT YOU CAN ADAPT THESE INSTRUCTIONS TO MAKE YOURS ANY SIZE YOU WANT.

Designer

●

Angela Kilby

INSTRUCTIONS

1 Make a photocopy of figure 1. Take it to the glass shop and have them cut acrylic sheet the same octagonal shape in a size of your choosing. If you wish to hang your sun catcher, have the shop drill a 1/4-inch (6 mm) hole, centered along a straight, outer edge and 1/2 inch (1.3 cm) in from the edge. Ask for some scraps of acrylic sheet, too.

2 As shown in figure 2 on page 54, use a pencil to trace lines on one side of the paper-covered octagon, creating an octagon in the center. Using the black marker, trace heavily over the center octagon.

3 Refer to figure 3 on page 54. Use the pencil and ruler to trace lines from the corners of the center octagon out to the opposing corners of the larger octagon. Go over the lines again with the permanent marker.

4 Turn over the octagon and peel off the unmarked paper backing. The marker lines should show through from the other side clearly enough to serve as a guide.

5 Practice applying the black fabric paint to a scrap piece of acrylic until you can apply it in a consistent, delicate line.

6 Lay the octagon flat on your work surface. Following the lines showing through the acrylic, use the fabric paint to outline the small octagon in the center of the sun catcher. Go over the lines connecting the small octagon to the periphery, then mark the outer edge of the octagon. Avoid smearing any wet lines. Wipe off any errors with a damp paper towel. Let dry overnight.

7 The colors are arranged in sequence to suit the nature of

TOOLS & MATERIALS

- **pattern on this page**
- **1/4-inch (6 mm) acrylic sheet cut into an eight-sided octagon shape, with the protective paper still adhered to both sides***
- **pencil**
- **metal-edged ruler**
- **black fine-tip permanent marker**
- **black, multi-purpose craft paint in a squeeze bottle with a small applicator tip**
- **scraps of acrylic sheet**
- **paper towels**
- **water**
- **1-ounce (28 gm) bottles of glass stain in the following colors: red, rose, lilac, white, Prussian blue, leaf green, dark green, purple, and light brown*****
- **paintbrush with a square tip**
- **toothpick**
- **scarlet silk cord (optional)**
- **small Oriental bell with tassel attached (optional)**

* **Glass and mirror suppliers usually sell sheet acrylic and will cut it to your specifications.**

*****Available at craft stores, in the section where premolded sun catcher shapes are sold**

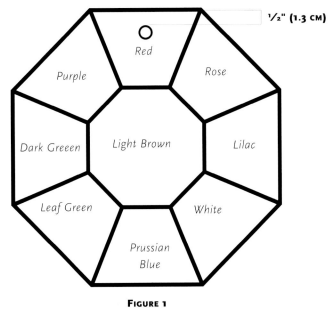

1/2" (1.3 CM)

Red
Purple
Rose
Dark Greeen
Light Brown
Lilac
Leaf Green
White
Prussian Blue

FIGURE 1

Perhaps as part of the belief that fish and amphibians bring luck, a statue of the three-legged money toad is often found in Asian homes and businesses. (Well, no one said a wealth attractor had to be pretty!) The money toad sits on a pile of coins and holds a coin in its mouth, too. Placed inside your front door so it faces toward the interior of the house, the toad invites more wealth to come.

each gua (fig. 1). Practice using the brush to apply a little glass stain to a scrap of acrylic. Now you'll paint the bagua. Pour a small quantity of glass stain in its designated section and quickly manipulate it with the brush, tilting the acrylic if necessary to direct the flow of the stain but staying inside the black lines. Use the toothpick to pierce any large bubbles. Try adding a little water to the brush, then swirling it in wet stain. Perfection is *not* desirable: Brush strokes, small bubbles, and variations in color intensity or texture create the look of old glass. Color all the sections and let dry overnight. If desired, add more color and let dry again.

Remove the paper backing. String the cord and bell through the hole if desired and knot them in place.

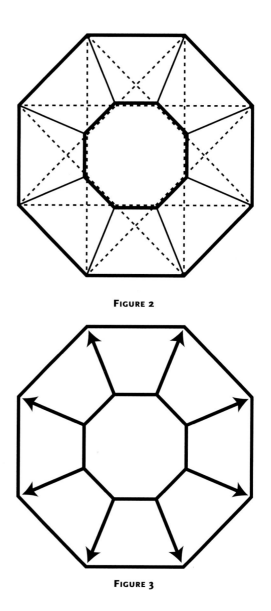

FIGURE 2

FIGURE 3

CHI BANNER

Whether you hang it from a ceiling beam to block cutting energy, float it in a window to entice chi, or hang it in a doorway to keep your home peaceful and secure, this spangled banner is both beautiful and powerful. Embellished with golden tassels and loose interpretations of auspicious ideograms representing Peace of Mind, Longevity, Double Happiness, and Wealth, the banner also incorporates a bamboo flute to assist with the upward flow of energy.

Designer

●

Jean Tomaso Moore

TOOLS & MATERIALS

- sheer, voile-type scarf, curtain panel, or yardage in a metallic bronze or copper color, 19 x 68 inches (48.3 to 172.7 cm)*

- 4 templates on page 57

- clear adhesive-backed paper, minimum amount 20 inches (50.8 cm) square

- masking tape

- paintbrushes in various sizes

- acrylic craft paints, 2 ounces (56 gm) each of black and ruby metallic

- paper towels

- scissors

- 34-gauge beading wire

- 30 grams of bronze-colored rocaille beads

- 50 gold spangles in 20-millimeter size

- 19-inch (48.3 cm) bamboo flute

- electric drill

- 7 1/2-inch (1.3 cm) screw eye hooks thread in a color to match the fabric

- sewing needle

- 2 gold tassels, 6 inches (15.2 cm) long

- 4 gold tassels, 3 inches (7.6 cm) long

- 2 yards (1.8 m) of 1/4-inch (6 mm) gold cord

* If using unfinished yardage, cut and hem to a finished size of 19 x 68 inches (48.3 to 172.7 cm).

56

INSTRUCTIONS

1 Use a photocopier to enlarge each of the four ideograms to a 5-inch-square (12.7 cm) size.

2 Adhere a 5-inch-square (12.7 cm) piece of clear adhesive-backed paper to each enlarged ideogram. Tape them to a large, flat work surface, spacing them evenly apart. Lay down the fabric panel over the centered images. Use tape to secure the fabric to the work surface.

3 Using a small paintbrush and the black acrylic paint, paint over one of the ideograms. Use a larger brush and the ruby metallic paint to paint a freehand box around the image. Use the paper towels to blot up excess ruby paint, leaving a very faint box around the ideogram. Repeat with the other ideograms. Let dry thoroughly, then remove the tape from the panel.

4 Use the scissors to cut thirty 4-inch (10.2 cm) lengths of the beading wire. Thread one rocaille bead onto each wire, making a knot to hold it in place. Add approximately 19 more beads to each wire.

5 Lay the panel flat on the work surface. Arrange the beaded strands symmetrically along the sides and bottom of the panel.

6 One by one, poke the tip of each beaded strand through the panel, knotting it from behind the panel to hold it in place.

7 Randomly lay the gold spangles onto the panel and use the the beading wire or needle and thread to sew them on, finishing with knots to hold the spangles in place.

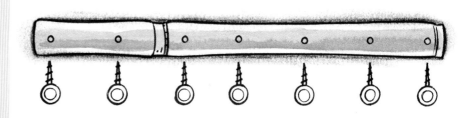

FIGURE 1

8 Lay the bamboo flute on its side, as shown in figure 1, and drill seven evenly spaced pilot holes along one side of the flute. Screw the screw eye hooks into the pilot holes.

9 Lay the 19-inch (48.3 cm) top edge of the fabric panel over the hooks, and use the needle and thread to sew the fabric to the eye hooks.

10 Tie a large tassel to the eye hook at each end of the flute by cutting the tassel's hanging cord in the center and threading each end between the flute and fabric, knotting it in the back around the hook (fig. 2). Tie the four smaller tassels across the center of the panel in the same fashion.

11 Cut a 2-foot (61 cm) length of the gold cording. Thread the cording through the flute, then tie the ends into a compact knot. Pull the knotted end back into the flute to hide the knot, and use the cord to hang the banner.

FIGURE 2

PEACE OF MIND

DOUBLE HAPPINESS

LONGEVITY

WEALTH

CORNER
CLOAKER
BANNER

**CREATED FROM A READYMADE
TABLE RUNNER, THIS STYLISH
BANNER IS THE PERFECT
SOLUTION FOR HIDING
CEILING OVERHANGS OR
CORNERS THAT GENERATE
CUTTING CHI. IF YOU CAN
WIELD A CRAFT KNIFE AND A
PAINTBRUSH, MAKING THIS
PROJECT
IS A SNAP.**

Designer

●

Terry Taylor

INSTRUCTIONS

1 Purchase a table runner to suit your taste. A design that incorporates several blocks of solid-color fabric will provide a good background for the embellishment.

2 Photocopy the template at lower right, enlarging it as needed for the areas you wish to decorate. The design shown in the photograph is 5³/₄ inches (14.6 cm) in diameter.

3 Lay the template on a flat surface suitable for cutting. Tape down the photocopied template, then tape the clear acetate over the template at each corner. Try to catch a little of the edges of both the photocopy and acetate.

4 Install a new, sharp blade in the craft knife and use it to cut out the stencil. Work slowly and carefully to achieve smooth cuts.

5 Place the stencil on the runner and tape the stencil down to prevent it from shifting as you work.

6 Apply some paint to the stencil brush, being careful not to overload the brush with paint. After dabbing the brush in the paint, use an up-and-down motion to "pounce" it on the sheet of newspaper. Continuing to use an up-and-down pouncing motion, lightly apply the fabric paint to the runner. If you'd like the paint coverage to be heavier, use the same technique to pounce additional paint on the fabric.

7 Leave the stencil in place until the paint dries, then pick the stencil straight up off the fabric and reposition it over the next area to be decorated.

8 Set the fabric paint according to the manufacturer's instructions.

9 Depending on whether you plan to hang the banner vertically or horizontally, use small stitches to sew the rings several inches apart on the "hanging" end or edge of the banner. Nail the brads or ornamental hooks in the wall and hang the banner.

MATERIALS & TOOLS

- **readymade table runner**＊
- **template shown below**
- **masking tape**
- **sheet of clear acetate**
- **craft knife and sharp blades**
- **fabric paint in metallic gold or another color of your choice**
- **stencil brush**
- **sheet of newspaper**
- **needle and thread**
- **small curtain rings**
- **small brad nails**
- **ornamental hooks (optional)**

＊**The runner shown measures about 1 x 5¹/₂ feet (30.5 cm x 1.6 m). Sale bins in bed and bath stores are a good place to find blank runners, especially after the winter holidays.**

CORNER PLANT SHELF

HOW MANY TIMES HAVE YOU HEARD THE FENG SHUI RECOMMENDATION TO USE
TRAILING PLANTS TO MASK PROJECTING CORNERS AND OTHER SOURCES OF
POISON ARROWS, ONLY TO GAZE FORLORNLY UPWARD AT A CORNER THAT
EXTENDS ALL THE WAY TO THE CEILING, WITH NOWHERE TO ATTACH A PLANT?
THIS LITTLE SHELF IS THE ANSWER. IF YOU HAVEN'T DONE WOODWORKING
BEFORE, HAVE AN EXPERIENCED FRIEND GUIDE YOU.

Designer ● Terry Taylor

INSTRUCTIONS

1 Measure and mark a 2-3/4 x 8-inch (6.9 x 20.3 cm) rectangle on the board. Measure and mark a 3-1/2 x 8-inch (8.9 x 20.3 cm) rectangle. Cut them out with the jigsaw. Set them aside.

2 Place the dinner plate on the remaining board. Trace around the board to create a circular shelf. Don't worry about making a complete circle. Cut out the shape. This shape will form the shelf.

3 Butt the smaller rectangle up against the wider (fig. 1) to form a right-angled form with equal sides. Use the wood glue and wood screws to secure the rectangles together. Drill two guide holes on each side of the rectangle assembly for the drywall screws. This will serve as the shelf support.

4 Set the shelf support upright on the circular shape, positioning the support at the back of the circular shape. Mark the interior angle of the support on the shelf. Use the saw to cut out the marked triangle.

5 Use wood glue and screws to attach the shelf to the support (fig. 2).

6 Paint the shelf as desired and attach it to the corner with the drywall screws.

TOOLS & MATERIALS

- 1 x 12-inch (2.5 x 30.5 cm) poplar board*
- pencil
- ruler
- jigsaw
- dinner plate
- wood screws
- wood glue
- drill and drill bits (optional)
- drywall screws**
- acrylic or latex paint

* Use scrap wood or purchase a 3-foot (91 cm) board

** Use screws that are appropriate for attaching the shelf to your wall, such as butterfly screws.

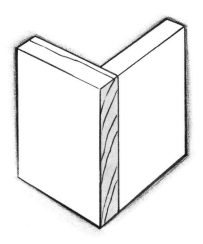

FIGURE 1

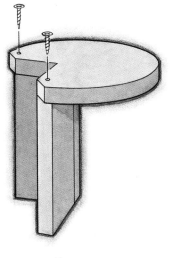

FIGURE 2

EARTH & CRYSTAL PLANT POT

FENG SHUI RECOMMENDS BALANCING THE EXTREMELY YIN WATER ELEMENT OF A BATHROOM WITH MORE YANG ENERGY, AND THE SNAKE PLANT SHOWN IN THE POT IS A FIRE ELEMENT PLANT IF THERE EVER WAS ONE! DISPLAY IT IN A POT YOU'VE EMBELLISHED WITH HAND-TIED MACRAME AND THREE CLEAR CRYSTALS.

Designer ● Terry Taylor

TOOLS & MATERIALS

- ceramic planter, about 3 feet (0.9 m) in circumference
- maroon and black cording, 3 yards (0.9 m) of each*
- hot glue gun and glue sticks
- 3 chandelier prisms**
- plant with spiky or pointed leaves, such as snake plant (*Sansevieria tri fasciata*) or Japanese blood grass (*Imperata cylindrica* 'Rubra')
- potting soil

* The circumference of the planter and of the cord affects the length of cord you need. The larger the planter and the thicker the cord, the more yardage required.

** Available in lamp shops and department stores

INSTRUCTIONS

1 This pot is embellished with two colors of cord tied in a knot pattern called an alternating half hitch. Refer to figure 1. Use one color of the cord to tie a half hitch over the cord of the other color, then switch, making the knot-bearing cord into the knotting cord. Tie another half hitch. Continue tieing and alternating cords until you have 3 to 4 inches (7.6 to 10.2 cm) of untied cord ends remaining.

2 Determine where on the planter you wish to attach the knotted cording and wrap it around the planter.

3 Hot glue the knotted cord to the ceramic at several points around the planter, making sure it doesn't sag between any glued points. Tie a knot in the free ends of the cords, centered on the front of the planter.

4 Slightly twist open the rings attached to the chandelier prisms and hang them from the cord, centering them on the knot.

5 Lower the plant into the pot and fill with the potting soil.

FIGURE 1

CHI WIND CHIME

WIND CHIMES ARE SAID TO "CALL IN CHI," LIFTING OUR SPIRITS WITH THEIR LOVELY SOUND, AND SOME FENG SHUI PRACTITIONERS BELIEVE THAT THE HOLLOW RODS OF THE CHIMES ATTRACT CHI, CHANGING BAD ENERGY INTO GOOD IN THE PROCESS. THESE CHIMES INCORPORATE A LARGE COIN TO ATTRACT GOOD FORTUNE, WHILE THE CRYSTALS BREAK LIGHT INTO THE RAINBOW SPECTRUM AND BRING BENEVOLENT YANG ENERGY. THE COLORS RED AND GOLD ALSO SIGNIFY HAPPY OCCASIONS. (DON'T YOU FEEL HAPPY JUST LOOKING AT THEM?)

Designer

●

Jean Tomaso Moore

PREPARING THE CHIME ELEMENTS

Note: Use the drill to lightly countersink all drilled holes to minimize abrasion on the cording.

1 Use the compass to draw a 4$\frac{1}{2}$-inch (11.4 cm) circle in the center of the 7-inch (17.8 cm) plaque. Use the tape measure and pencil to mark and draw two pencil marks 1$\frac{1}{2}$ inches (3.8 cm) apart at the twelve, two, four, six, eight and ten o'clock positions on the outer edge of the 4$\frac{1}{2}$-inch circle.

2 Put on the safety glasses (always wear them when drilling or cutting). Drill holes into each of these points, using the $\frac{1}{8}$-inch (3 mm) bit. The chime rods will hang from this area.

3 Drill four additional $\frac{1}{8}$-inch (3 mm) holes $\frac{3}{4}$ inch (1.9 cm) in from the edge of the plaque at the twelve, three, six, and nine o'clock positions. Cord will be placed in these holes to help balance the chimes.

4 Drill a $\frac{1}{2}$-inch (1.3 cm) hole through the center of the plaque. The wind catcher, the clapper cording, and the chime hanging cord will be threaded through this hole.

5 Sandwich and glue together the three smaller wooden disks, clamping them together until the glue sets. Drill a $\frac{1}{8}$-inch (3 mm) hole through the center of the sandwich, which will serve as the chime clapper.

6 Sand and prime all wooden pieces. When the primer dries, paint them with the copper acrylic.

7 Use the grease pencil to mark the following lengths on the copper pipe: 16$\frac{5}{8}$, 17$\frac{5}{8}$, 19$\frac{1}{4}$, 20$\frac{7}{16}$, 21$\frac{5}{8}$, and 23$\frac{3}{4}$ inches (42.2, 44.8, 48.9, 51.9, 54.9, and 60.3 cm). Use the pipe cutter to cut the pipe to these lengths or have them cut at a local home improvement center.

8 Working from the shortest to the longest rod, measure and mark the following distances, one per rod: 3$\frac{1}{2}$, 3$\frac{3}{4}$, 4, 4$\frac{1}{4}$, 4$\frac{1}{2}$, and 5 inches (8.9, 9.5, 10.2, 10.8, 11.4 and 12.7 cm). Drill the holes all the way through each rod. Use the metal file to smooth cut edges and to remove any burrs from drilled areas, including inside the rods.

9 Gently sand the entire surface of each rod to create a burnished look. Remove any dust residue, then spray the clear acrylic sealer on the rods. Let dry.

10 Drill a $\frac{1}{8}$-inch (3 mm) hole $\frac{1}{2}$ inch (1.3 cm) from the bottom of the large brass coin. The coin will serve as the chime's wind catcher. Thread a short piece of the red satin cord through the hole to

MATERIALS

- **1 unfinished circular wooden pine plaque, 7-inch (17.8 cm) diameter**٭
- **3 unfinished wooden pine disks, 2-$\frac{1}{2}$-inch (6.4 cm) diameter and $\frac{1}{4}$ inch (6 mm) thick**٭
- **carpenter's wood glue**
- **wood primer**
- **2 ounces (56 gm) copper metallic acrylic craft paint**
- **10 to 11 feet (3 to 3.3 m) of copper pipe, $\frac{1}{2}$-inch (1.3 cm) outer diameter**
- **clear mat acrylic spray sealer**
- **ornamental brass "fortune coin," 6-$\frac{1}{4}$ inches (15.8 cm) in diameter** ٭٭
- **10 yards (9 m) red satin (also called rattail) cord**
- **10 yards (9 m) monofilament, in 25-pound (11.4 kg) strength**
- **1 large red double tassel** ٭٭
- **8 crystal prisms, 3 inches (7.6 cm) long**٭٭٭
- **20 to 30 glass beads, in a mixture of red and clear**
- **2 red wooden beads, 1-inch (2.5 cm) diameter**
- **10$\frac{1}{4}$-inch (6 mm) brass screw eyes**٭
- **ceiling hook**

٭ **Sold at craft stores**

٭٭ **Sold by Feng Shui retailers on the Internet**

٭٭٭ **Available in lamp departments or hardware stores**

SEE NEXT PAGE FOR TOOLS & SUPPLIES

- compass
- tape measure
- lead pencil
- safety glasses
- power drill with ⅛-inch (3 mm), ½-inch (1.3 cm), and countersink bits
- wood clamp
- entra-fine sandpaper
- paintbrush
- grease pencil
- pipe cutter or hacksaw (optional)
- metal file
- scissors
- cellophane or masking tape

attach the double tassel, tying several knots to hold it in place.

11 Cut six 30-inch (76.2 cm) lengths of monofilament. Thread a 3-inch (7.6 cm) crystal pendant onto the bottom of each of four strands, tying several knots to hold each crystal in place. Add several glass beads of various shapes and colors along the length of each strand of monofilament, knotting them in place.

12 Thread beads onto the remaining two strands of monofilament, knotting in place.

THREADING THE CORD THROUGH THE CHIMES AND ATTACHING THE CLAPPER

1 Cut four 30-inch (76.2 cm) lengths of satin cord. Fold each cord, knotting its ends to create a double thickness for added strength. These cords will be used to balance the chimes from the top when all other parts are in place.

2 Cut another length of cord 90 inches (228.6 cm) long, folding it in half to create a double thickness. Working from the top side of the large plaque, run the two strands of the doubled cord through the large opening in the center of the plaque, leaving 12 inches (30.5 cm) of cord on the top side of the plaque. Make a knot. (This excess cord will help balance and hang the chimes.) Make another knot on the underside of the plaque.

3 Wrap the cord's ends with a piece of tape, twisting it into a needlelike shape, then thread the cord through the clapper.

4 Place a wooden bead on the cord, allowing both the clapper and bead to hang 12 inches (30.5 cm) from the plaque, then make a double or triple knot under the bead to hold the clapper in place.

5 About 7 inches (17.8 cm) down the cord make another knot. Allow another ½ inch (1.3 cm) and knot again. From this point on, you'll be working with the single ends of the cord.

6 Wrap the cord ends around the center opening of the large coin (fig. 1). Knot each end of the cord four or five times at the top of the coin, positioning the coin so it hangs evenly (fig. 2).

HANGING THE COPPER RODS

1 Cut 50 inches (127 cm) of cord. Wrap one end with the tape to facilitate threading. You'll now hang the rods in sequence according to length.

2 From the top side of the plaque, pull the cord all the way through one hole (designated for the rods). Knot the end several times to hold the cord in place.

3 Working from right to left, thread the other end of the cord through the first, longest rod. Bring up the end of the cord and thread it through the next hole drilled into the 7-inch (17.8 cm) plaque. Then thread the cord back down through the next hole and through the holes in the next-longest rod. Again, pull the cord up and thread it from the underside through the next hole in the plaque.

4 Continue to thread all the rods, allowing each one to hang about 1½ to 2 inches (3.8 to 5 cm) from the bottom of the plaque. Rearrange the cords on each rod to balance the chimes as much as possible at this stage, hanging them so that the clapper falls about midway between all the rods. Make sure the longest rod is raised high enough so it doesn't hit the wind catcher.

5 When all the rods are threaded and arranged, run the end of the cord up through the remaining hole and make several knots to hold in place.

1 Thread the four lengths of double-thick, 15-inch-long (38.1 cm) cord through the four extra holes, working from the underside of the plaque and allowing the knots to remain on the underside. Tape the ends of the cord to facilitate threading.

2 Gather together the four new cords and the extra 12-inch (30.5 cm) length of cord that was already threaded through the center of the plaque. Tape their ends together and thread them through the second wooden bead. Allow the chimes to hang and adjust the cords so the chimes are balanced.

3 Make a large knot to hold the five sets of cords in place.

4 Screw in the eye hooks at symmetrical points on the underside of the 7-Inch (17.8 cm) plaque. Thread each strand adorned with a crystal and beads through the screw eyes, allowing the strands to hang at varying lengths. Tie several knots in the monofilament at the hook to hold in place.

5 Screw more eye hooks on the inside of the plaque at the twelve, three, six, and nine o'clock positions. Hook one crystal prism onto each screw eye. Your wind chime is now ready to hang. Screw in the ceiling hook and do so!

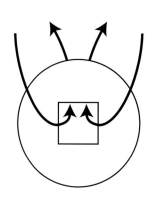

FIGURE 1

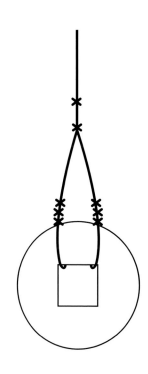

FIGURE 2

EASY
MIRROR
COVER

**IF YOU HAVE A FAVORITE
DRESSER WITH A MIRROR IN
YOUR BEDROOM, THIS IS A
STYLISH BUT EASY WAY TO
COVER THE MIRROR AT NIGHT,
PROMOTING A MORE RESTFUL,
YIN ATMOSPHERE.**

Designer ● *Jane Wilson*

INSTRUCTIONS

1 Measure from the topmost point of the mirror to the bottom. Mark that length on both sides of the panel, then use the ruler to draw a straight line between the two marks. Cut along the straight line. (This way, you preserve the existing hem on the panel.) Set aside the excess fabric.

2 Tape the wrapping paper behind the top of the mirror and use the marker to trace its outline down to the points where the straight, parallel sides of the mirror begin (fig. 1). If the mirror is rectangular, extend the outline down along the sides at least $4\frac{1}{2}$ inches (11.4 cm). Cut out the template.

3 Center the template on the top, raw edge of the curtain panel. Pin in place. Make a pencil outline of the template on the fabric. Remove the template and cut out the outline, adding $\frac{1}{2}$ inch [1.3 cm] around the edge for seams.

4 Iron under $\frac{1}{4}$ inch (6 mm) along the panel sides. Iron under another $\frac{1}{4}$ inch. Stitch in place.

5 Lay the fabric you reserved in step one flat on the work surface and lay the template on top. Pin in place and cut out a piece of fabric the same shape and dimensions as the template, adding $\frac{1}{2}$ inch (1.3 cm) for seams along the edges. Remove the pins. This will form a "pocket" for hanging the mirror cover.

6 Pin the pocket cutout to the curtain panel, right sides together, and stitch together using a $\frac{1}{4}$-inch (6 mm) seam. Leave the side seams open to allow for some "give" in the fit of the cover to the mirror. Remove the pins.

7 To add shaping seams to the cover, turn the fabric assembly inside out. At the top point of the cover, pinch the cover right sides together and sew a seam straight across (fig. 2), aligning the seam so it connects the seam allowance, raw selvage edges, and fabric of the pocket and cover. Make the shaping seam at least as deep as the mirror is thick. Use the same technique to add another two shaping seams 10 to 12 inches (25.4 to 30.5 cm) on each side of the first shaping seam.

8 Turn the cover right side out and press out any wrinkles.

TOOLS & MATERIALS

- tape measure
- chalk or pencil
- 1 floor-length, sheer or semi opaque curtain panel*
- ruler
- scissors
- wrapping paper or any other long piece of paper
- masking tape
- black fine-tip permanent marker
- straight pins
- iron
- thread to match the curtain panel
- sewing machine

* If you're covering a small mirror, you may be able to use a cafe-length panel. Check the dimensions and adapt the instructions.

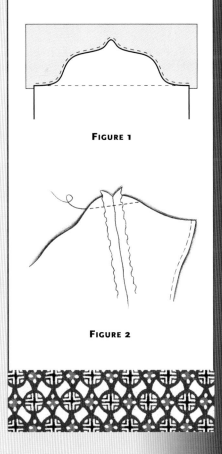

FIGURE 1

FIGURE 2

PHOENIX MIRROR WITH SHUTTERS

If, like most of us, you use your bedroom as a dressing room, too, you've probably got a mirror on the wall. Yet Feng Shui tells us that mirrors can interfere with restful sleep, especially a mirror that reflects the bed. Here's how to adapt a ready-made mirror so you can "put it to bed at night" by closing its shutters. It's also decorated with a glorious Celestial Phoenix.

Designer

●

Cathy Smith

1 Measure the frame opening on the mirror, and measure, mark, and cut two door panels from the wood panelling to fit.

2 Measure and mark the positions where the four hinges will be installed, approximately 5-1/2 inches (14 cm) from the top and bottom of the frame. Using a hinge as a template, lightly trace around it onto the wood.

3 At the positions marked for the hinges, use the craft knife to cut out insets on the inner lip of the frame, so each hinge will be flush with the inner surface of the frame.

4 Sand the panel doors, smoothing away any roughness. Fit the doors inside the frame and mark hinge positions on the doors. Remove the doors, drill holes in the frame and doors for screwing in the hinges, and attach the hinges.

5 Hang the doors on the frame, checking their fit. Measure and mark where the pulls and latch will be installed. Remove the doors, drill holes for the knobs and latch assembly, and screw them in. Rehang the doors, checking alignment, then remove the latch assembly and pulls, leaving the doors attached to the frame.

6 Measure the embossed wood trim to fit the closed doors. Use the miter saw to miter the corners of the trim and cut off any

- **wall mirror with simple wooden frame**⁕
- **wooden panelling, 18¹⁄₂ x 26³⁄₄ x ¹⁄₂ inch (47 x 67.9 x 1.3 cm)**
- **4 brass hinge assemblies with screws**
- **2 cabinet pull knobs**
- **brass latch and hasp assembly**
- **embossed wooden trim, 81 inches (205.7 cm)**
- **4 decorative wood rosettes, 1¹⁄₂ inches (3.8 cm) square**
- **wood stain in a color to match the mirror frame**
- **pattern on page 72**
- **oil-based craft paints in blue, green, orange, and red**
- **rub-on metallic gold accent paint**
- **spray polyurethane**

⁕**The one shown in the photo measures 22¹⁄₄ x 30¹⁄₄ inches (56.4 x 76.8 cm).**

SEE NEXT PAGE FOR TOOLS & SUPPLIES

- **tape measure**
- **pencil**
- **handsaw or jigsaw**
- **craft knife**
- **sandpaper**
- **power drill**
- **flat-head screwdriver**
- **miter box and saw**
- **carpenter's glue**
- **C-clamps**
- **2-inch (5 cm) paintbrush**
- **carbon paper**
- **masking tape**
- **hammer**
- **³⁄₄-inch (1.9 cm) finish nails**
- **#0 round paintbrush**
- **#6 round paintbrush**
- **turpentine**
- **rags**

excess trim at the points where the doors meet.

7 Use the carpenter's glue to adhere the trim to the doors, making sure the mitered corners join closely. Clamp in place and let the glue set. Glue the rosettes in place and let dry.

8 Brush a coat of the wood stain over the doors, trim, and rosettes. Let dry.

9 Enlarge the pattern at lower left to fit the doors. Lay the carbon paper face down on the doors; lay the pattern on top so it's centered between the latch assembly and knobs, and tape in place. Trace the pattern, transferring it to the doors.

10 Carefully detach the doors (with hinges still attached) from the frame, and hammer the finish nails into the trim at 5-inch (12.7 cm) intervals to further secure it.

11 Use the brushes and oil-based craft paint to color the phoenix as desired. First, use black to outline the design and let dry, then apply the color. Add a subtle stripe of orange on the inner edge of the embossed wood trim, add color highlights to the rosettes, and rub the gold accent paint on the trim and rosettes as desired. Let dry. Use the turpentine to clean the brushes.

12 Keeping the (still detached) doors flat on the work surface, spray on two coats of polyurethane. Let dry.

13 Rehang the doors on the mirror frame.

ORNAMENTAL FLOOR RUNNER

SOME FENG SHUI PRACTITIONERS POSITION RUGS TO LEAD CHI FROM ROOM TO ROOM, AND YOU CAN DO THE SAME WITH THIS PROJECT, A SIMPLE SISAL RUNNER STENCILLED WITH A BOLD CHINESE MOTIF.

Designer ● Terry Taylor

TOOLS & MATERIALS

- **template on page 59**
- **sheet of clear acetate**
- **masking tape**
- **sharp craft knife**
- **black acrylic paint**
- **textile medium***
- **small container**
- **stencil brush**
- **sisal runner**
- **newspaper**

*This medium is available in the paint section of most craft stores.

INSTRUCTIONS

1 Photocopy and enlarge the stencil template on page 59 so it measures 9 inches (22.9 cm) across. Place the photocopy under the sheet of clear acetate. Tape the photocopy to the acetate. Use the craft knife to cut out the stencil.

2 Mix the paint and textile medium in a small container in the proportions recommended by the manufacturer.

3 Place the stencil on the runner. Use a few strips of tape to secure the stencil to the runner.

4 Load your stencil brush by dabbing it in the paint

mixture. Use an up-and-down, "pouncing" motion. Pounce the brush on the newspaper until only a trace of paint shows. It's better to stencil with a lightly loaded brush. You can always apply more paint; you can't take off paint.

5 Stencil the motifs on the rug as desired. The motifs on the rug shown in the photograph are alternated from side to side and are placed about 1½ inches (3.8 cm) from the margin of the rug and in the center. Let the stencils dry.

Six-Sided Lucky Coin Chandelier

Designer ● *Cathy Smith*

A CHANDELIER IS ONE OF THE GREAT YANG ENERGIZERS OF FENG SHUI DECORATING,
ADDING BRILLIANT FIRE AND STRONG EARTH ENERGY. FIRE ALSO FEEDS EARTH,
AND EARTH FEEDS THE METAL ELEMENT. THE CLEVERLY PUNCHED METAL BODY OF
THIS FIXTURE IS CREATED FROM READY-MADE PANEL ANCHORS FROM THE HOME
IMPROVEMENT STORE AND FEATURES THE ALWAYS LUCKY COIN SYMBOL AND
LUXURIOUS HAND-TIED AND BEADED TASSELS. HANG YOUR CHANDELIER
IN THE FIRE OR EARTH SECTORS OF A ROOM.

CREATING THE BASIC CHANDELIER SHELL

1 Photocopy the punch pattern (fig. 7 on page 77), enlarging it to fit the panel anchors as shown in figure 2.

2 Mark, measure, and cut six pieces of the sheet metal, 4$^1/_4$ x 8 inches (10.8 x 20.3 cm). Cut six 8-inch (20.3 cm) pieces of the panel anchor. Note that the pattern on the panel anchor isn't symmetrical; cut the six pieces so their perforations follow the same pattern along the edge. That way, you can "match up" the perforations when assembling the chandelier. Cut six 5$^3/_4$-inch (14.6 cm) pieces of the metal cleat. If you'd prefer not to do the cutting, have a local metal fabricating shop do it for you.

3 Securely tape the edges of the six sheet metal panels to the wooden board. Center the punch pattern on the metal and tape it down. Be sure to leave a $^1/_2$-inch (1.3 cm) margin along the top and bottom.

4 Use the awl and hammer to punch the pattern onto the metal. Before removing the pattern, make sure all the holes are punched. Repeat with the other five panels. If the sheet metal starts to curl, hand flatten it after you finish punching.

5 Now you'll bend the metal cleats to create a hexagon frame for the panels. Clamp a 5-$^3/_4$-inch (14.6 cm) piece of cleat in the vise with half the cleat in the vise. Use the hammer to bend the cleat along its length to

create an angle slightly less than 90° (fig. 1).

FIGURE 1

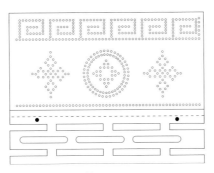

FIGURE 2

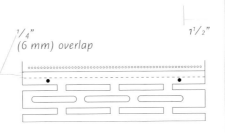

$^1/_4$"   1$^1/_2$"
(6 mm) overlap

FIGURE 3

ATTACHING THE PANEL ANCHOR STRIP TO THE PUNCHED METAL

1 Clamp the panel anchor very firmly onto a horizontal wood surface (the steel is tough and you want to make sure it can't move). Using the $^1/_8$-inch (3 mm) bit, drill two holes in the top section of the panel anchor 1$^1/_2$ inches (3.8 cm)

MATERIALS

- **pattern on page 77**
- **sheet metal, 16 x 14 inches (40.6 x 35.6 cm)**
- **4 panel anchors, 1$^3/_4$ x 24 inches (4.4 x 61 cm)**
- **sheet metal cleat, 1 x 40 inches (2.5 x 51.6 cm)**
- **steel bar stock, 2 x 18 x 1/16 inch (5 x 45.7 cm x 1.6 mm)**
- **ceiling lighting fixture✲**
- **swag lamp kit✲**
- **automotive door edging**
- **6 feet (1.8 m) of silver chain, cut into 12-inch (30.5 cm) lengths**
- **12 open S-hooks, 1 inch (2.5 cm) long**
- **removable link**
- **6 15m skeins of #3 perled cotton, 3 blue and 3 black**
- **fancy glass beads, large teardrops, and prisms, 6 each**
- **metallic beads in a variety of shapes and colors**
- **car pinstriping tape, $^1/_8$-inch-wide (3 mm) red and $^1/_4$-inch-wide (6 mm) black**

✲ **If you'd prefer not to wire the chandelier yourself, take it to a local lamp shop**

SEE NEXT PAGE FOR TOOLS & SUPPLIES

TOOLS & SUPPLIES

- ruler or tape measure
- pencil or black fine-tip permanent marker
- metal shears
- masking tape
- wood board
- awl
- hammer
- vise
- screwdriver
- drill with 1/8, 1/4, and 3/8-inch (3, 4, and 9.5 mm) bits
- 40 bolts, 3/32-inch (2.4 mm) diameter and 1/4 inch (3 mm) long
- 40 nuts to fit the bolts
- hacksaw
- pliers
- scissors
- beading wire
- 2 ceiling hooks

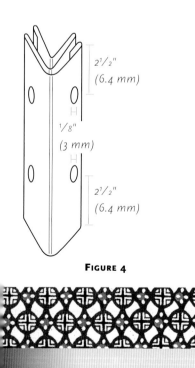

FIGURE 4

from each end (fig. 2). When drilling metal, it may be easier to use the 1/8-inch bit to start holes.

2 Refer to figure 3 on page 77. Center the drilled panel anchor over the punched metal so the top 1/4 inch (3 mm) of the panel anchor overlays the bottom 1/4 inch of the punched panel. Drill through the sheet metal panel at the same location as the hole drilled in the panel anchor.

3 Use a bolt and nut to attach the sheet metal and panel anchor. Repeat this process with the other five sides and panel anchors.

ATTACHING THE ASSEMBLED PANELS TO THE CLEATS

1 Refer to figure 4. Drill 1/8-inch (3 mm) holes in the 5 3/4-inch (14.6 cm) cleat length. For clarity, we'll call one end of the cleat the bottom. From the bottom end of the bent cleat, drill two holes on either side of the bend 2 1/2 inches (6.4 cm) above the bottom edge and 1/8 inch (3 mm) in from the outer edge of the cleat. From the top end, drill two holes on either side of the bend 1 1/2 inch (3.8 cm) from the top edge and 1/8 inch in from the outer edge of the cleat.

2 Slide the punched metal panel, its front side facing the outer bend of the cleat, into the cleat, butting the edge of the panel all the way against the corner in the cleat. Drill holes into the panel in the same places as those drilled in the cleat and connect them with bolts and nuts. Repeat for each

panel until all sides are joined and bolted.

3 Using the 1/4-inch (3 mm) drill bit, drill a hole in the top and bottom of each cleat corner about 3/8 inch (9.5 mm) from the top and bottom edges.

SETTING UP AND WIRING THE LIGHTING FIXTURE

1 Using the 1/8-inch (3 mm) bit, drill two holes each in two opposing panels as follows: Center the holes from the side edges of the panel, 1 inch (2.5 cm) apart and 3/8 inch (9.5 mm) down from the top edge of the panel.

2 Measure the diameter of the hexagon. Use the hacksaw to cut the steel bar stock the measurement of the diameter plus 2 3/8 inches (5.95 cm).

3 Place 1/2 inch (1.3 cm) of one end of the cut steel bar in the vise, and bend the end to a 90° (curved) angle. Refer to figure 5. Measure the bar, starting from the outside of the curved end to the diameter of the hexagon. Add 3/16 inch (5 mm) and mark. Place the mark at the edge of the vise clamp and secure, then bend the bar into a 90° angle. Check to make sure the bar fits in the hexagon. Adjust if necessary, and cut off excess, leaving a 1/2-inch (1.3 cm) leg to bolt to the shell. Using the holes drilled in the shell, mark the holes in the bar stock and drill.

4 Find the center of the bar stock and mark. Secure the bar and use the 3/8-inch (9.5 mm) bit to

drill a hole in the center. Follow the instructions with the ceiling fixture and swag lamp kit to wire your lamp, or take it to a lamp shop and have it wired.

ADDING THE CHAIN

1 Before installing the S hooks in the cleat corners to hold the hanging chain and tassels, apply the automotive door edging to the top rim of the lamp. Piece it together, if necessary, beginning and ending in the middle of a panel. Cover any gaps with some of the black auto pinstriping material.

2 Attach the 12-inch (30.5 cm) lengths of chain to one end of the S hooks and use the pliers to close the hook end. Put the other ends of the hooks through the holes drilled in the tops of the cleat corners and use the pliers to close the hooks.

3 Hang the chandelier from the swag chain (the other chains are for balance and decorative effect). Position the unattached ends of the silver chains so they're even with a link in the swag chain. The chains should be straight and free of tension, and the lamp should be level. Use the removable link to attach the chains to the swag.

EMBELLISHING THE LAMP

1 To make simple tassels, remove the paper wrapper from the perled cotton skein (a skein is a doubled loop twisted together). Untwist the skein and open it up. Untie the ends. Leaving the skein in a loop, unravel one end four times, giving you about 4 feet (1.2 m) of thread. Cut the thread from the skein.

2 Use the scissors to cut a 12-inch (30.5 cm) piece of thread, fold the skein in half and then in half again. Run a 10-inch (cm) thread through the fold and, with the thread ends even, tie it tightly at the skein fold.

3 About 1 inch (2.5 cm) from the top of the tassel, tie the remainder of the thread, leaving a 3-inch (7.6 cm) tail at one end. Wrap the long end of the thread around the tassel, coiling it tightly upward, toward the top of the tassel, covering 1/4 inch (3 mm) of the skein (this will be about 12 wraps).

4 Start wrapping the thread downward, coiling it tightly until the thread end reaches the 3-inch (7.6 cm) tail. Tie the tail and the other end together tigntly in a double square knot, and clip the ends about 1/4 inch (3 mm) away from the knot.

5 Cut the thread loops at the bottom of the tassel and trim evenly. String a bead onto the doubled thread at the top of the tassel, and knot the thread securely at the top.

6 Hang the beaded tassel from the S hook and hook it into the hole drilled at the bottom corner of the cleat. Close the S hook. Make and hang three blue and three black beaded tassels.

7 String assorted glass beads on a double strand of the beading wire. End the strand with a large, teardrop-shape bead or prism. Retain a 1-inch (2.5 cm) section of the strand at the top for hanging the beads. Make a total of six beaded strings.

8 Use the 1/8-inch (3 mm) red pinstriping to create accent lines above and below the Chinese coin symbol on the panel. Use the 1/4-inch (6 mm) black pinstriping on the bottom edge of the panel anchor, cutting off the pinstriping at the edge where the panel and cleat meet.

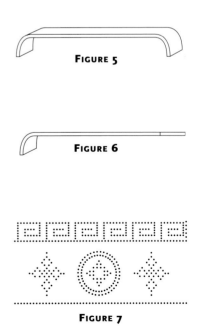

FIGURE 5

FIGURE 6

FIGURE 7

FAUX BRONZE BUDDHA

DO YOU WANT TO GET CHI'S ATTENTION BY ADDING A GORGEOUS BRONZE SCULPTURE TO YOUR LIVING SPACE, BUT YOU CAN'T AFFORD THE LARGE PRICE TAG? IT'S EASY TO PAINT AN INEXPENSIVE CONCRETE GARDEN STATUE SO IT LOOKS LIKE IT'S MADE OF OLD METAL. EVEN CHI WILL BE FOOLED!

Designer
•
Janice Eaton Kilby

Instructions

1. Cover your work surface with the newspaper and set the figurine on top. Apply a coat of primer and let dry.

2. Mix a dark, metallic green undercoat by putting about half of the green paint in a container and adding a few squirts of red paint. Use a craft stick to mix them together, adding more red to darken the green if desired. Mix in a little bronze paint, then swirl in a little more but don't mix it in thoroughly.

3. Paint the figurine with the green mixture and let dry. Lightly load the brush with black paint and brush it on, working it into the crevices and detail areas of the figurine. Use the sponge, rag, or your fingers to wipe away excess paint. Don't attempt to make the paint perfectly even; old bronze contains many color variations and mottled hues. Let dry.

4. Add a tiny bit of blue, green, and yellow to white paint to create a very light blue-green hue, and apply it sparingly to places on the statue where, in your mind's eye, a metal statue would have been corroded by the elements.

Wipe away the excess and let dry. Add bronze highlights to prominent points on the statue that a viewer might touch: the nose, hands and belly, for example. Let dry.

5. Add water to some of the white paint and brush it over some of the surfaces to tone down the color and make it look old. Wipe away most of it and let dry.

6. If you'd like to display your statue outdoors, apply the clear sealer and let dry.

Tools & Materials

- **newspaper**
- **concrete figurine**✶
- **white latex primer**
- **2-inch (5 cm) paintbrush**
- **2-ounce (56 gm) bottles of acrylic craft paints in metallic Christmas green, bright red, metallic solid bronze, black, blue, yellow, and white**
- **clean, empty plastic containers**
- **wooden craft sticks**
- **assorted, stiff-bristled artist's paintbrushes**
- **sponge or rags**
- **spray-on clear acrylic sealer (optional)**

✶**Available at garden supply centers. The statue shown in the photograph is about 18 inches (45.7 cm) tall.**

Before and After: A Real-Life Feng Shui Makeover

Since most of us can't afford to build the perfect Feng Shui house from scratch, we have to figure out how to work with what we've got. After reading about common Feng Shui problems in chapter 2, you're now aware that there are plenty of attractive, inexpensive ways to improve your home's Feng Shui. Here's a before-and-after survey of the Feng Shui makeover of a real-life home.

This two-story, 1,600-square-foot (144 sq m) house is set on a wooded hillside. The main entrance is on the top floor and faces the upslope of the hillside, a Feng Shui no-no. A deck surrounds two and a half sides, and visitors must ascend stairs without risers to get to the front door.

The house contains three bedrooms and two

baths, plus a few other rooms. Fortunately for the residents, it was already a symmetrical rectangle in shape. Two dogs and three cats added plenty of yang energy when the family wasn't home.

But the most frequently used rooms in the house suffered from many Feng Shui problems. The main entrance on the top floor of the house opens directly into a Great Room containing cooking, dining, and living areas with no walls to separate them, plus an overpowering fireplace and a high, sloped cathedral ceiling that chi could get lost in! The windows are a bit too small to let in much light for a room this size. And even worse, the front door stands in direct line with a pair of glass doors on the other side of the house. Chi came in one door and flew straight out the other. The kitchen cabinets and large open bookshelves had the potential to create lots of cutting chi, too.

The upstairs bathroom was about as anti-Feng Shui and overwhelmingly yin as it gets. Small and windowless, it completely lacks any natural light and air, and its only colors were white,

beige, and pale pastels. Dismal!

A rather bare stairwell led to the lower floor. The stairwell contained one small wall lamp and an eight-sided window (fortunately, an auspicious shape). The small master bedroom is located on the lower floor with, again, problem ceilings with slopes and lots of sharp angles, plus a projecting inner corner that made the room L shaped. A large glass window and door take up most of one end of the room.

But a little thought about what chi loves—light, color, and life—and an inexpensive but imaginative application of paint, plants, textures, and accessories has worked wonders for this home's energies! Read on to see how they did it.

Front Door and Entryway

Cover the window with a semi-opaque curtain to slow down chi.

■ Install a tall light in the back-yard, or a weather vane or other ornament on the roof, to lift chi and balance the front and back slopes.

■ Reconfigure the house layout so the front door is on the floor level of the side of the house which faces the downslope. This solution wasn't feasible in this particular case, so the homeowners built foot-high (30.5 cm) walls of interlocking brick to form half-circles outside the two downstairs doors, then planted them with flowers. The walls will

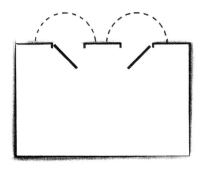

help keep chi from gushing out the downstairs doors.

■ Position a screen or room divider to shield at least part of the fireplace from the view of someone walking in the door.

Problem

The bland, uninviting front door has a window insert that lets chi barge through. The steps leading up to the door have no risers, so chi has trouble even making it up to the door. The front door also faces the upslope of a mountain. Since a home's main entrance is referred to as the "mouth of chi," these are serious problems. The lack of division between front door, fireplace, and kitchen also means any chi which enters will be "burned up" or dissipated.

Solutions

■ If you're bold, paint the front door red or another bright color to attract chi.

■ Position pots of bright flowers on both sides of the door and on the steps.

■ Add risers to backs of steps if at all possible.

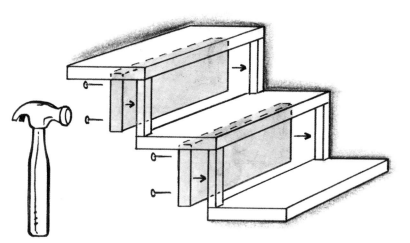

LIVING ROOM

To make your own beautiful statue to get chi's attention, see the Faux Bronze Buddha project on page 78. Directions for making the Double Happiness Screen are on page 113.

Problem

Alignment of front door with glass doors that survey an attention-getting view encourages chi to rocket straight through room and out of the house.

Solutions

■ Position furniture to interrupt path of chi between front and back doors.

■ Position trees or a screen in front of glass doors.

■ Place bright objects and attention-getting art in chi's path.

■ Hang sheers over glass doors.

■ Position a wind chime in the path of the doors, or hang a mirror on the wall above the glass doors.

Problem

Colors are bland and natural light is subdued.

Solutions

Paint is the cheapest Feng Shui fix! Consult the bagua on page 24 for colors appropriate for the area of the house to be energized. Cooling green was added to the walls to balance the overpowering fireplace

Fu Dogs, like the pair shown here, are traditional protectors of the Feng Shui energies of a home. Position them at waist level or higher on either side of your front door or gate leading into your property.

Hang banners or other decorations from the ceiling to symbolically separate the entry, living room and kitchen. Position plants on the countertop to further separate the spaces.

The owner refurbished a pair of muted blue table lamps by painting them antique red and gold and adding new Oriental-style shades.

An Open Book

This homeowner came up with an ingenious solution to avoid cutting chi created by open bookcases

Before the shelves were installed, a router was used to shape the corners and edges so they're slightly curved. (Ask a friend who knows woodworking to help you.) Taste and budget permitting, another solution would be to install matchstick blinds or soft fabric shades over sections of the bookcase.

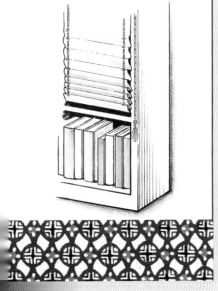

and calm the Fire element of the kitchen.

- Add art, wind chimes, and colorful, glimmering pillows and throws to attract chi. Hang crystals in the windows.

Problem

Sloping ceilings compress chi and create feeling of heaviness.

Solutions

Add tall plants and torchère lamps to encourage chi to move upward toward ceiling.

Problem

The fireplace (and therefore Fire element) dominates the room.

Solutions

Fireplace implements were removed and the Fire element calmed with Earth by placing ceramics on the mantelpiece and river rocks and a large plant in the hearth. (The TV has also been hidden in a cabinet.)

BATHROOM

Problem

This bathroom has no windows and no natural light. The color scheme, fixtures, and linens are bland and colorless. There's nothing here to attract chi!

Solutions

■ Do everything possible to bring more light into the room. Sponge or rag-paint the walls a rich, textured color. The walls shown in the photograph were first painted with a maize gold base coat, allowed to dry, then a red glaze was applied by hand. Materials are easily found at any home improvement center.

■ Spray-paint the shower curtain rod and rings a bright metallic color or another vibrant color of your choice.

■ Dye the shower curtain and seat cover a rich color. Glue or stitch light-catching decorative trim to the curtain.

■ Purchase inexpensive but richly colored towels, and stitch on ready-made, metallic-embroidered trim to add sparkle. (If you don't sew, use fusible webbing or fabric glue.) The trim design shown is called Greek Key.

■ Position plants with pointed leaves in ceramic pots flanking the toilet to increase Fire and Earth elements. Wicker containers will also increase Wood element, which moderates Water. Place a couple of substantial rocks in the space under the tank to ground chi.

Add a plant to the countertop and a small, low-wattage lamp that always stays on.

85

See page 64 to learn how to make your own beautiful Chi Wind Chime.

STAIRWELL

Problem

Since chi acts like water, it will quickly fall from the living room on the upper floor to the bottom of this rather bare stairwell.

Solutions

■ Hang art on the walls, and hot-glue faceted crystal trim to a simple clip-on lamp shade to create a light source that's irresistable to chi!

■ The pottery collection on display adds more Earth element to help feed the wood siding on the walls.

■ Abundant, brightly colored flowers also invite chi to slow down (just be sure to keep silk ones dusted).

■ Position a mirror to grab chi's attention at the top of the stairs.

■ Install chimes or a sun catcher in a window to catch light and add color. See page 52 for directions to make your own Bagua Sun Catcher.

BEDROOM

Problem

This bedroom was located in the Wealth area of the home, but its decor was rather bare and the colors neutral. It did have the benefit of tall, wooden furniture crafted with flowing lines and curved edges, including a bed with a solid headboard and footboard (optimal, in Feng Shui terms). But uncovered windows allowed chi to rush in and out, creating an unsettled atmosphere.

Solutions

A bedspread and lined draperies were created from inexpensive Indian bedspreads. Their intricate patterns and rich violets, greens, blues, and reds produced a luxurious effect. Pillows in touch-me textures, such as chenille and velvet, were also piled on the bed to enhance the yin atmosphere.

Problem

Sloping ceilings compress chi, creating an intense as opposed to a restful atmosphere.

Solutions

The room was painted a deep, restful green around its perimeter to blend in awkward angles and to "lift" the white, sloped ceiling. Dimmer spotlights in the ceiling are turned on to activate chi and encourage it to move upward. Plants aren't usually recommended as bedroom decoration because of

the lively yang energy they add to what should be a restful yin environment. But the homeowner felt the acute feeling of compression caused by the sloped ceilings in her bedroom called for drastic action—and she likes plants! Chimes were also hung to interrupt cutting chi.

Problem

The vanity mirror facing the bed prevents restful sleep, as did a television (not shown).

Solution

Cover the mirror at night (see Easy Mirror Cover, page 68). The TV was removed to another room, but if you don't want to banish yours, cover it at night, too.

Problem

The Relationship area of this bedroom, the most intimate room of the house, sorely lacked anything to show that a couple lives here.

Solutions

A group of romantic images were hung on the wall in the Relationship sector along with a pair of mandarin duck figurines, symbols of love.

4

Beautiful How-To Projects for All Parts of the Bagua

Now that you understand how all the pieces of Feng Shui work together and culminate in the bagua, it's time to move from your head to your heart.

How does your home feel to you? Is it a place of refuge, a serene oasis with things to delight the eye? What is life like now for you and your loved ones? Is your work going well? How happy are your personal relationships? Would you like to change some aspect of your life? Keeping those answers in mind, go ahead and match your living space to the bagua of your choice, as explained on pages 23 through 26.

Hopefully you've already dealt with any of the common structural problems explained in chapter two. Now, starting with the sector of the bagua called Life's Path or The Journey, this chapter explains each area of the bagua in more detail. After Life's Path, come the sectors of the bagua called Knowledge, Health and Family, Wealth, Fame, Relationship, Children and Creativity, Helpful People and Travel, and the Center, the point of connection of all other sectors of the bagua and the source of harmony and balance. Which parts of your life, and therefore of the bagua, do your feelings tell you need attention and assistance?

Once you've identified the bagua sectors you want to energize, you can pick one of the projects in chapter two (page 32) or choose from the projects in the following pages. In this chapter, the projects are grouped by bagua sector and are made in the appropriate colors, shapes, materials, and finishes that support and strengthen the sector's elemental energies. Dozens of easy-to-adapt templates of good luck symbols, decorative patterns, and ideograms to embellish your projects are also included. Would you rather minimize the energies in a sector? No problem! Consult the Weakening Cycle on page 18, then pick a project made with a calming element.

For example, do you wish you had more recognition for the work you do? Then add Fire objects to the Fame sector or "feed" the fire with Wood objects. Do you seek mystical enlightenment or a deeper knowledge of self? Locate the Helpful Beings and Travel sector and decorate it with images of holy teachers or spiritual beings. Would you like to draw closer to your significant other? Replace any solo objects with pairs of things in the Relationships sector. Are your children driving you crazy? Add the calming Water element to the Children and Creativity sector. That's how it works.

Among the dozens of auspicious patterns and motifs you can use to embellish your projects, you'll see designers' interpretations of many Chinese ideograms, including the ideograms for happiness, longevity, and wealth. Please note that true Chinese calligraphy is an art perfected by many years of practice, and the meanings of the ideograms depend on precision. If it's important to you that an ideogram be correct down to the last brush stroke, consult with a trained calligrapher. Otherwise, feel free to enjoy the process of decorating your home with evocative symbols that help you visualize and remember the good things in life.

Feng Shui is not a rigid straightjacket, so be flexible and try different things. Whatever choices and changes you make, keep an open mind, pay attention to the results, and make corrections as needed. As the world's many different wisdom traditions teach us, the point is for us to enjoy our journey!

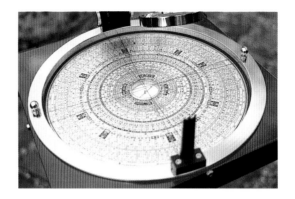

LIFE'S PATH OR
THE JOURNEY

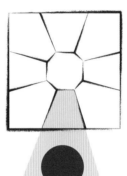

ELEMENT ▪ WATER

I CHING TRIGRAM ▪ WATER

COMPASS DIRECTION ▪ NORTH

MOVEMENT OF CHI ▪ FLOWING

SHAPES ▪ FREE-FORM

COLORS ▪ BLACK, BLUES, AND DARK COLORS

MATERIALS ▪ GLASS AND WATER

IMAGERY ▪ FISH, FROGS, WATER FEATURES SUCH AS WATERFALLS AND RIVERS

Where are you going with your life? Do you have a sense of direction, or are you seeking to know the special gifts and destiny you are here to realize? Are you making important changes in your livelihood, the way you make a living? The Life's Path sector of the bagua, also known as The Journey, influences this aspect of your life. Like the serenely flowing water evoked by the colors, shapes, and materials of Life's Path, energizing this aspect of the bagua puts you in touch and in harmony with your true purpose.

YIN/YANG TABLE SHRINE

WHETHER YOU SEEK PEACE, AFFIRMATION, OR MEMORIES OF YOUR LOVED ONES, THIS TABLE SHRINE PROVIDES A SIMPLE YET BEAUTIFUL FOCUS FOR YOUR MEDITATIONS. WHILE THE MIRROR SYMBOLIZES WATER ELEMENT SMOOTHLY FLOWING UNDER A CALM SURFACE, THE YIN/YANG MOTIF SERVES AS A TIMELESS REMINDER OF LIFE'S CYCLE OF LIGHT AND DARK, PAST AND PRESENT.

Designer

●

Jean Tomaso Moore

MATERIALS

- 11 x 14-inch (27.9 x 35.6 cm) unfinished pine frame, constructed with 2-inch (5 cm) wooden sides
- 1 x 8 pine board*
- 6 wood screws, 1³⁄₄ inches (4.4cm) long
- 4 straight top plates with screws (used to attach feet to shelf)
- 4 wooden feet, 2¹⁄₂ inches (6.4 cm) high, with screw inserts
- primer paint
- 2 ounces (56 gm) red acrylic craft paint
- gold acrylic spray paint
- pattern on page 93
- 11 x 14-inch (27.9 x 35.6 cm) mirror
- rubbing alcohol or glass cleaner
- paper towels
- clear adhesive-backed paper
- 3 ounces (84 gm) glass etching cream
- 11 x 14-inch (27.9 x 35.6 cm) piece of lightweight cardboard
- glazier's points (used to set panes of glass)
- 2 eye hooks (optional)
- picture-hanging wire (optional)

*Note that these dimensions are standard industry specifications; the actual width is 7¹⁄₄ inches (18.4 cm). If you haven't done woodworking before, get an experienced friend to help you or have the board cut at your local wood shop

INSTRUCTIONS

1 Measure and mark a 14-inch (35.6 cm) length on the 1 x 8 pine board. Use the jigsaw to cut it off.

2 Butt the bottom of the unfinished pine frame to the top of the pine board. Create the altar shelf by using the drill and the 1-³⁄₄-inch (4.4 cm) screws to attach the board to the frame.

3 Screw the top plates to the corners of the bottom of the shelf, then screw the feet into the top plates.

4 Sand all surfaces to smooth out any rough spots. Also sand the corners of the frame and shelf to create slightly rounded edges. Wipe with the tack cloth.

5 Use the foam brush to apply primer to the entire piece. Let dry, then paint on a coat of the red acrylic. Let dry. Spray all surfaces with the gold paint.

6 Using a photocopier, enlarge the yin/yang pattern to approximately 5 inches (12.7 cm) in diameter.

7 Use the paper towels and alcohol or glass cleaner to clean the surface of the mirror. Let dry.

8 Cover the entire surface of the mirror with the clear adhesive-backed paper, smoothing out any bubbles as you go.

9 Decide on the placement of the symbol on the mirror. In the etching process, all of the areas where the clear adhesive-backed paper is removed will be etched, so pay close attention to figure 1 and follow steps 10 and 11 very carefully.

10 Set the circle cutter at 5 inches (12.7 cm) and use it to cut into the contact paper. Adjust the cutter again to 5¹⁄₄ inches (13.3 cm) and make a second cut. Peel off the ¹⁄₄-inch (6 mm) strip of clear adhesive-backed paper you just created (A in fig. 1).

11 Use the circle cutter or craft knife to cut out a 1-inch (2.5 cm) circle, and peel off the contact paper to expose the mirror (B in fig. 1). Cut the second 1-inch circle where indicated, but leave the contact paper in place on the mirror (C in fig. 1). Make another cut on the left side of the design, but leave this small border of clear adhesive-backed paper in place (D in fig. 1) to preserve a sliver of unetched mirror that will help outline the design. Finally, use the craft knife to cut out the shaded area in the diagram. Peel away the clear adhesive-backed paper from the shaded area (E in fig. 1), leaving the small circle and small border strip on mirror.

12 Before etching, use the paper towels and alcohol or glass cleaner to clean the exposed areas of the mirror.

13 Use the foam brush to apply a very thick layer of the etching creme on the exposed areas of the mirror. Allow to set for 24 hours, then wash away the cream as directed on the packaging and peel off the remaining adhesive paper. Clean the entire surface of mirror again to remove any adhesive or etching creme residue.

14 Insert the mirror into the frame. Place the 11 x 14-inch (27.9 x 35.6 cm) piece of cardboard on the back of the mirror to protect the surface from scratches.

15 Now you'll install the glazier's points to secure the cardboard backing and mirror to the frame. Lay the mirror face down. Lay the points flat and on top, all around the circumference of the mirror. Use the tip of the flat-head screwdriver to push the points into the frame.

16 If desired, the shrine can be made into a wall piece by unscrewing the feet. Screw the two eye hooks to the back and add the picture hanging wire.

TOOLS & SUPPLIES

- **tape measure**
- **pencil**
- **jigsaw**
- **power drill**
- **power screwdriver**
- **sandpaper**
- **tack cloth**
- **foam brush**
- **paintbrush**
- **circle cutter**✷
- **craft knife**
- **flat-head screwdriver**
- ✷ **Available at craft stores**

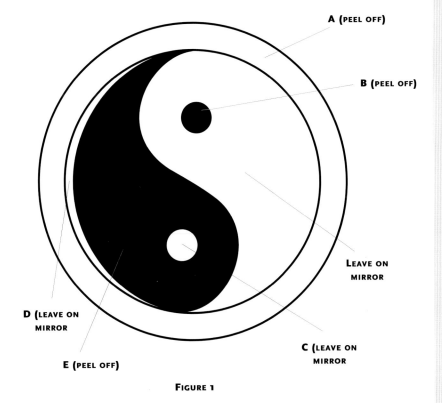

A (PEEL OFF)

B (PEEL OFF)

LEAVE ON MIRROR

D (LEAVE ON MIRROR)

E (PEEL OFF)

C (LEAVE ON MIRROR)

FIGURE 1

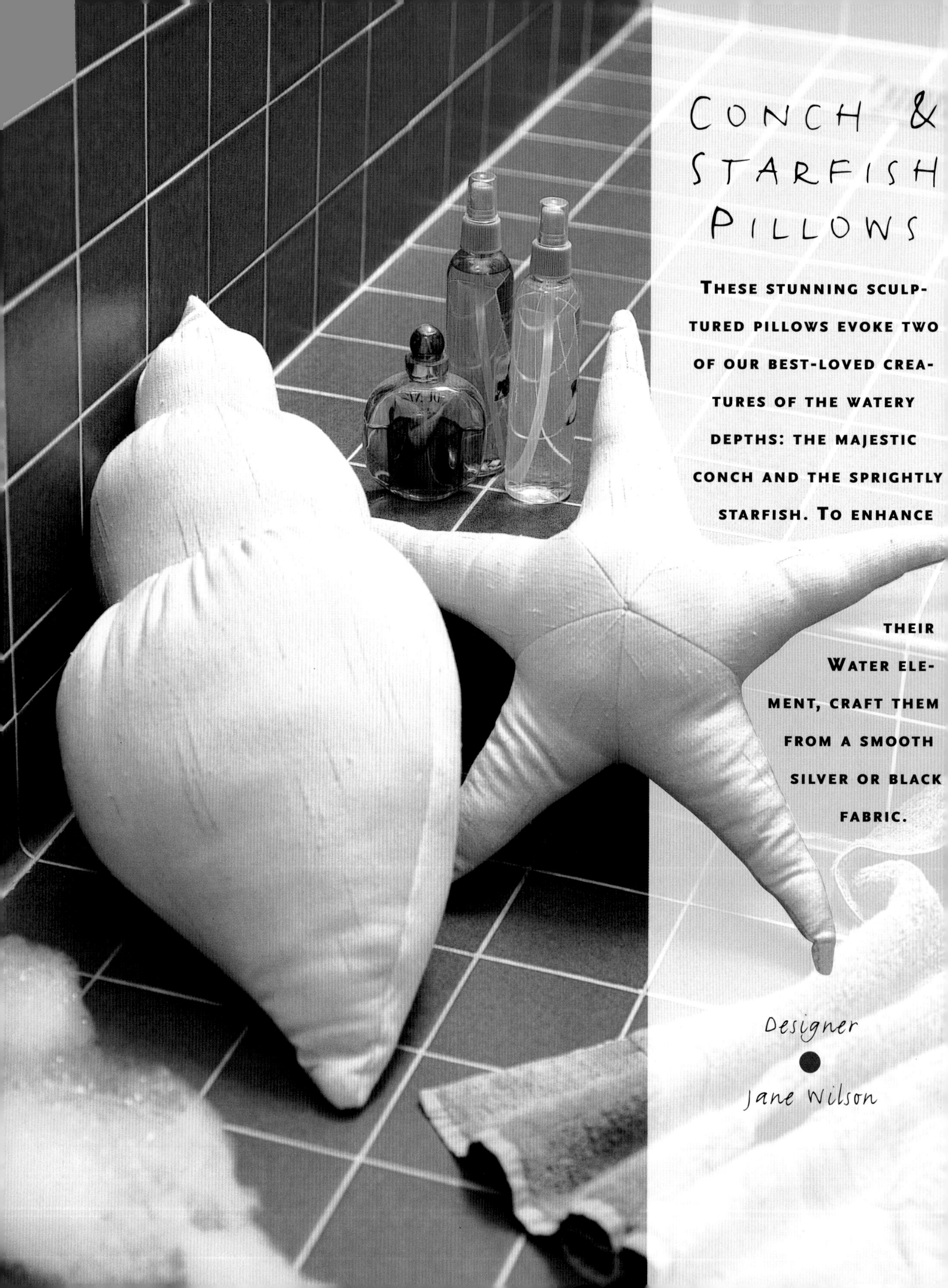

CONCH & STARFISH PILLOWS

THESE STUNNING SCULP-TURED PILLOWS EVOKE TWO OF OUR BEST-LOVED CREA-TURES OF THE WATERY DEPTHS: THE MAJESTIC CONCH AND THE SPRIGHTLY STARFISH. TO ENHANCE THEIR WATER ELE-MENT, CRAFT THEM FROM A SMOOTH SILVER OR BLACK FABRIC.

Designer
●
Jane Wilson

INSTRUCTIONS

1 Right sides together, fold the largest piece of fabric at its midpoint. Pin the two 17-inch (43.2 cm) ends together and use a 1/2-inch (1.3 cm) seam to sew them together (fig. 1 on page 96). Leave a 4-inch (10.2 cm) opening at the top for stuffing. Remove the pins and iron the seam open. Repeat with the 7 x 2-inch (17.8 x 5 cm) and 12 x 4-inch (30.5 x 10.2 cm) pieces.

2 Cut a flattened half-circle out of the 4 x 2-inch (10.2 x 5 cm) piece, as shown in figure 2 on page 96.

3 By hand or using a basting stitch on your machine, gather one 31-inch (78.7 cm) raw edge of each section (fig. 3 on page 96). Still working with right sides together and matching up the seams, pin the gathered edge of the largest piece to the ungathered edge of the medium-size piece, and use a ¹/₂-inch (1.3 cm) seam to join then. Repeat, seaming the straight edge of the smallest section to the gathered edge of the medium section. The seam of the lowest, largest section should still contain the 4-inch (10.2 cm) opening for stuffing.

4 Right sides together, create a cone out of the flattened half-circle of fabric, right side in, and use a ¹/₄-inch (6 mm) seam to join

the edges together. Pin and sew it to the top, gathered edge of the conch assembly. Remove the pins.

5 Refer to figure 4 on page 96. Lay the inside-out assembly flat, manipulating the fabric so the original seam (A) of the lowest, largest section of the assembly lies in the center. Draw the lower outlines of the conch as shown to guide shaping seams. Reposition the fabric so seam A lies to the left (fig. 5 on page 96), and stitch a shaping seam along the line drawn to the right, tapering it off about 5 inches (12.7 cm) below the "shoulder" of the conch. Flip the fabric around again and sew a shaping seam along the second line you drew, stopping it about 4 inches (10.2 cm) below the other shoulder of the conch (which will be more prominent when stuffed). Remove the pins.

6 Trim the seam allowances, clip curves, and press the seams open, including the edges of the opening left for stuffing the pillow.

7 Turn the pillow right side out and stuff it, then sew the opening closed by hand.

TOOLS & SUPPLIES

Required for Both Projects

- **sewing machine**
- **straight pins**
- **iron**
- **sewing needle (optional)**
- **scissors**
- **pencil or chalk**

MATERIALS

- **1 yard (0.9 m) of fabric in color of your choice, cut into four pieces measuring 31 x 17 inches (78.7 x 43.2 cm), 7 x 2 inches (17.8 x 5 cm), 12 x 4 inches (30.5 x 10.2 cm), and 4 x 2 inches (10.2 x 5 cm) respectively**
- **matching thread**
- **3 pounds (1.4 kg) polyester fiber fill stuffing**

PATTERNS FOR STARFISH LEGS

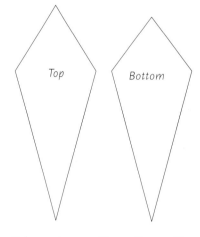

Top   *Bottom*

Enlarge pieces 200%, another 200%, then 125%. Add ¹/₄" (6 mm) seam allowances when cutting out pieces.

MATERIALS

- patterns for top and bottom of starfish legs on page 95
- 1 yard (0.9 m) fabric, in the color of your choice
- matching thread
- pencil, chopstick, or knitting needle
- 1 pound (0.5 kg) polyester fiber fill stuffing

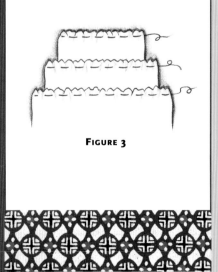

FIGURE 1

FIGURE 2

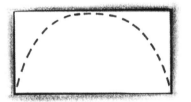

FIGURE 3

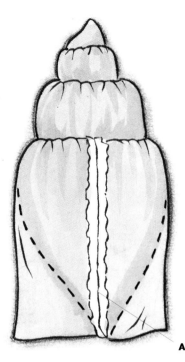

FIGURE 4

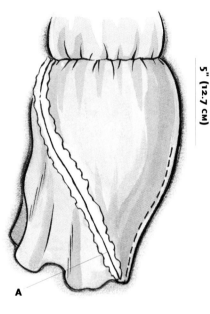

FIGURE 5

5" (12.7 CM)

4 Turn the starfish right side out. Stuff the pillow, using the pencil, chopstick, or knitting needle to poke the stuffing into the "points," and sew the opening closed by hand.

INSTRUCTIONS

1 Enlarge the patterns as directed. Pin the patterns to the fabric and cut out five top pieces and five bottom pieces. Remove the pins.

2 Right sides together, sew together the five top pieces by using a 1/4-inch (4 mm) seam to join their two shorter edges (fig. 5), creating a star shape. Repeat with the five bottom pieces, leaving one seam open, as indicated on the pattern, to allow you to stuff the pillow.

3 Fit the top and bottom assemblies right sides together, matching up edges. Pin in place. Stitch them together along their longer edges, using a 1/4-inch (6 mm) seam. Remove the pins.

GLASS TABLETOP FOUNTAIN

BOTH GLASS AND WATER ARE APPROPRIATE FOR THE LIFE'S PATH GUA, AND THIS GRACEFUL TABLETOP FOUNTAIN COMBINES BOTH. IT'S MADE FROM A SIMPLE GLASS LIGHT FIXTURE COVER AND OTHER MATERIALS EASILY FOUND AT HOME IMPROVEMENT STORES AND AQUARIUM SUPPLIERS.

Designer ● Marthe Le Van

TOOLS & MATERIALS

- **submersible pump**
- **clear plastic tubing, to fit pump spout and light fixture hole**
- **glass bowl with squared sloping edges, 3 x 12 inches (7.6 x 30.5 cm)**
- **nonweight-bearing, opaque white collar with three notches for pump cord and water circulation**
- **glass light fixture cover, molded and etched with a spiral pattern and scalloped edge, 4 x 8 inches (10.2 x 20.3 cm) or smaller than glass bowl**
- **utility scissors or sharp knife**
- **pieces of tumbled glass**
- **glass half marble**

INSTRUCTIONS

1 Set the pump's water flow regulator to the lowest setting. Place the clear plastic tubing over the pump spout, forming a tight seal. Position the pump on the base of the bowl, with the spout at the center. Conceal and protect the pump with the collar, making sure no fountain element rests directly on the pump.

2 Feed the tubing through the hole in the light fixture cover. Slide the light fixture down the tube to rest on the interior sides of the glass bowl; the pump's electrical cord passes under the scalloped edge of the light fixture. (The scalloped edge also permits the falling water to circulate back into the bowl.)

3 Cut the plastic tubing flush with the top of the hole in the light fixture cover. Telescope the tubing if needed to produce a tight fit with the light fixture's hole.

4 Pour water slowly through the gap between the glass bowl and light fixture. Add enough water to the bowl to cover the pump's intake valve.

5 Use the tumbled glass to cover the area where the glass bowl and light fixture meet. Turn on the pump to check the water flow. Place the glass half marble on top of the light fixture's hole to soften the jet and evenly distribute the water around the glass. Adjust pump pressure as needed.

KNOWLEDGE OR WISDOM

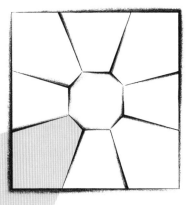

ELEMENT EARTH

I CHING ▪ TRIGRAM MOUNTAIN

COMPASS DIRECTION ▪ NORTHEAST

MOVEMENT OF CHI ▪ DOWNWARD

SHAPES ▪ NO FIXED FORM

COLORS ▪ DARK GREENS AND BLUES, BLACK

MATERIALS ▪ PLASTER, CHINA, CLAY, CERAMIC, BRICK, NATURAL FIBERS, SOFT STONES SUCH AS SANDSTONE, CRYSTALS, SEMIPRECIOUS STONES

IMAGERY ▪ PEONIES, CRANES, PINE TREES, BAMBOO, MOUNTAINS, DEITIES AND HOLY BEINGS

MUCH LIKE THE DOWNWARD MOVEMENT OF ITS EARTH ENERGY, THE KNOWLEDGE SECTOR OF THE BAGUA INFLUENCES OUR SEARCH FOR DEEP INNER WISDOM. THIS IS THE SECTOR WHERE THE ENERGIES OF OUR TEACHERS AND SPIRITUAL GUIDES HELP US. IT'S AN EXCELLENT LOCATION FOR A PERSONAL SHRINE OR A COLLECTION OF OBJECTS THAT HAVE SPIRITUAL MEANING TO YOU. LEARNING TOOLS, SUCH AS A **TV**, COMPUTER, OR BOOKS ARE ALSO GOOD FOR THIS LOCATION. AVOID WATER ELEMENT, BECAUSE IT COMBINES WITH THE SECTOR'S DOMINANT EARTH ELEMENT TO CREATE MUD, THE VERY OPPOSITE OF CLEAR THOUGHT AND FEELING.

WISDOM JOURNAL & PEN SET

BAMBOO IS A SYMBOL OF LONGEVITY TO THE CHINESE, AND THIS LOVELY JOURNAL IS EMBELLISHED WITH A TEXTURED MOTIF OF THE DURABLE EVERGREEN PLANT. USE IT TO RECORD YOUR DREAMS AND THOUGHTS AT TIMES OF QUIET CONTEMPLATION. IT'S EASY TO MAKE YOUR OWN BAMBOO-COVERED PEN, TOO, TO ENHANCE WOOD ELEMENT.

Designer  *Lynn Krucke*

INSTRUCTIONS

1 Cover the front and back of the journal with the handmade paper, cutting it to fit. Lap a margin of paper inside the edges of the journal, and glue the paper in place. Set aside to dry.

2 Place a piece of the stencil plastic over the bamboo pattern below and trace it with the fine-tip marker.

3 Using the craft knife, carefully cut out the stencil.

4 Center the stencil on the mat board. Holding stencil and board firmly in place, use the craft knife or palette knife to spread the stencil paste evenly across the stencil. Make sure the paste fills the stencil openings but don't let it squeeze under the edges of the stencil.

5 Lift the stencil straight up and wash it immediately. When the stenciled image has dried, paint the mat board including the raised image with one or two coats of black paint.

6 Using your finger, pick up some of the metallic rub-on paint and highlight the raised image and the edges of the mat board "tile." Let dry.

7 Cut a coordinating piece of the card stock so it's slightly larger than the tile. Glue the tile on top. Let dry, then mount it on the front of the journal.

8 Replace the original binding of the journal, threading the ribbon through the holes and tying it tightly over the chopstick. If your journal isn't bound this way, glue the ribbon and chopstick to the front of the journal.

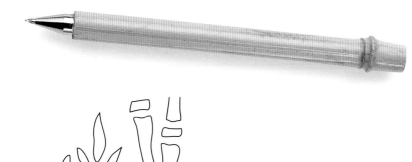

MATERIALS

- **purchased journal**⁎
- **exotic or handmade paper**
- **glue stick or other adhesive suitable for paper**
- **stencil plastic**
- **bamboo pattern on this page**
- **black fine-point permanent marker**
- **mat board**
- **stencil paste**
- **wooden craft stick or palette knife**
- **black acrylic paint**
- **metallic rub-on paint**
- **card stock scraps in coordinating colors**
- **chopstick**
- **ribbon**
- **craft glue or epoxy**
- **inexpensive stick-style ball-point pen**
- **hollow piece of bamboo, about 6 inches (15.2 cm) long, its inner diameter large enough to accommodate the ball-point pen barrel**
- **clear acrylic varnish**
- ⁎ **The book shown in the photo measures 5³/₄ x 6³/₄ inches (14.6 x 17.1 cm). There are many sizes and styles of blank books available. Alter the directions to fit your choice. A spiral-bound book will accommodate the ribbon and chop stick binding.**

TOOLS & SUPPLIES

- **scissors**
- **craft knife**
- **cutting mat, magazine, or other work surface**

Pyramid Crystal Light Box

A GLORIOUS CRYSTAL MERITS A SPECIAL PRESENTATION, AND THIS DISPLAY BOX CON-
TAINS A LOW-WATTAGE BULB THAT ILLUMINATES FROM BELOW. **I**T'S CONSTRUCTED
MUCH LIKE THE ANCIENT STEPPED TEMPLES KNOWN AS AS ZIGGURATS. **C**RYSTALS ARE
EXCELLENT FOR ACTIVATING **E**ARTH ENERGY, SO CHOOSE YOUR OWN TO TOP THE BOX.

Designer ● Jane Wilson

INSTRUCTIONS

1 Glue the equal lengths of wood together, forming five squares. Lay them on the waxed paper and let dry.

2 Paint the wood assemblies. Use several coats of the black enamel paint and let dry between coats.

3 Assemble the box by stacking the successive layers of wood, as shown in figure 1, glueing each stack in place. Let dry. Turn the stack upside down and glue a wooden bead to each corner (to serve as feet). Let dry, then paint the beads black.

4 Apply the rub-on gold acrylic paint to the exterior of the light box, and use the rag to quickly wipe off the excess. Let dry, then use the polystyrene foam to wedgr the light fixture into place inside the wood assembly. To avoid a fire hazard, make sure the light bulb doesn't touch the foam or wood.

5 Top with the crystal.

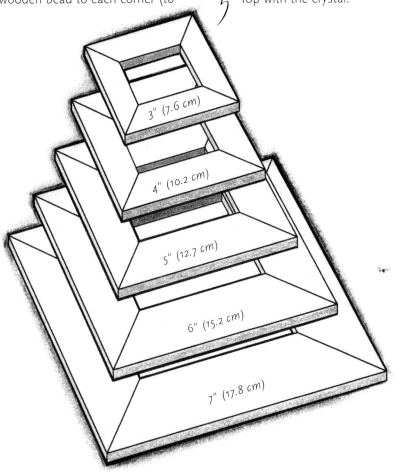

FIGURE 1

3" (7.6 cm)

4" (10.2 cm)

5" (12.7 cm)

6" (15.2 cm)

7" (17.8 cm)

TOOLS & MATERIALS

- **2 pieces of 1 x 2 lumber❋, each 8 feet (2.4 m) long, or 120 inches (3 m) of simple molding, cut to the following dimensions:**
    - **4 pieces, each 3 inches (7.6 cm) long on the longest side**
    - **4 pieces, each 4 inches (10.2 cm) long on the longest side**
    - **4 pieces, each 5 inches (12.7 cm) long on the longest side**
    - **4 pieces, each 6 inches (15.2 cm) long on the longest side**
    - **4 pieces, each 7 inches (17.8 cm) long on the longest side**
- ❋ **Refer to figure 1 on this page and use the miter box and saw to cut to the dimensions specified, or have the piece cut at a local wood shop.**
- **miter box**
- **saw**
- **wood glue**
- **waxed paper**
- **black gloss enamel paint**
- **paintbrush**
- **4 wooden beads, 1-inch (2.5 cm) diameter**
- **single light fixture with 7-watt bulb and on/off switch❋**
- **metallic gold rub-on paint**
- **clean rag**
- **2 pieces of polystyrene foam, each measuring 1 x 3 x 1 inch (2.5 z 7.6 x 2.5 cm)**
- **crystal❋❋**

❋ **Stores selling Christmas decorations stock these bulbs.**

❋❋ **Crystals that contain flecks, bubbles, and imperfections capture the light more beautifully than a perfectly clear gem.**

PAINTED PEONY TEA SET & NAPKINS

You've probably seen simple white teapots and cups like these in many an Asian restaurant. It's easy to paint a tea set and napkins using images of the peony, considered by the Chinese to be a symbol of love, affection, and feminine beauty. The ceramic material of the tea set enhances Earth element.

Designer ● *Jane Wilson*

INSTRUCTIONS

1 Photocopy the peony patterns below, reducing or enlarging as needed to fit the teapot, cups, and napkins.

2 Position the stencil plastic over a photocopy and use the marker to trace the pattern. Make a separate stencil for each color used in a design: one for the sections of blossom (rose) and one for the leaves (green). Repeat for each pattern.

3 Practice using the craft knife to cut curves on a piece of scrap stencil paper, then secure the stencils by taping them on top of the magazine or cut-proof surface. Now, cut out the color sections of the stencils, removing only the sections to be painted green in one

stencil and only the rose sections in the complementary stencil.

4 To follow classic stencil painting technique, lightly load the brush with the ceramic paint, dab the brush onto a paper towel until it's almost dry, and "punch" the brush through the stencil. Or, you may wish to use light paint strokes for a different effect. Tape a stencil to the teapot in the desired location, apply the paint, and let dry. Remove the stencil, then tape the stencil for the second color in place. Apply paint and let dry. Repeat to embellish the teacups. Repeat with the napkins and fabric paint, following the manufacturer's directions to set the paint. Use the marker to outline the patterns.

TOOLS & MATERIALS

- **white ceramic teapot and cups**✻
- **patterns shown below**
- **stencil plastic**
- **black fine-point permanent marker**
- **masking tape**
- **magazine or cut-proof work surface**
- **craft knife with new blade**
- **air-drying paints made for ceramic or porcelain, in deep rose and green**
- **stencil brush**
- **paper towels (optional)**
- **white fabric napkins**
- **fabric paints, in deep rose and green**
- ✻ **Found at Asian groceries and import shops**

TEAPOT

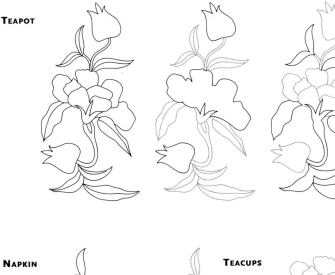

NAPKIN

TEACUPS

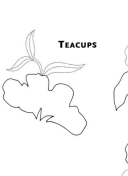

HEALTH AND FAMILY OR COMMUNITY

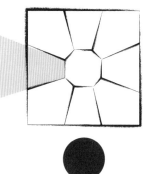

ELEMENT ▪ **WOOD**

I CHING TRIGRAM ▪ **THUNDER**

COMPASS DIRECTION ▪ **EAST**

MOVEMENT OF CHI ▪ **UPWARD**

SHAPES ▪ **TALL, SQUARE, OR RECTANGULAR SHAPES**

COLORS ▪ **GREENS, BLUES**

MATERIALS ▪ **WOOD, WICKER, RUSH, BAMBOO, PAPER**

IMAGERY ▪ **TREES AND PLANTS, DRAGONS, FAMILY PICTURES**

Asian cultures venerate their ancestors as continuing sources of good fortune and wisdom. You, too, should honor your own past and present family members by placing their images in the Health and Family sector of the bagua. The upwardly reaching Wood energy of this sector is supported by wooden furniture, especially tall, rectangular pieces such as cabinets or shelves. Keep any yellow or red hues to a minimum and avoid placing metal objects in this sector (if you can't, add an element that calms Metal energy).

FAMILY PHOTO WALL HANGING

THIS LOVELY WALL HANGING IS A WONDERFUL FUSION OF FAR EASTERN REVERENCE FOR FAMILY AND THE MOTIFS AND COLORS ASSOCIATED WITH WOOD ELEMENT. MAKE IT WITH PHOTOCOPIES OF TREASURED ANTIQUE PHOTOGRAPHS OR MORE CONTEMPORARY IMAGES.

Designer ● Lynn Krucke

MATERIALS

- 12 pieces of mat board, each 4 inches (10.2 cm) square
- exotic and handmade papers in shades of blue and green
- glue stick or other adhesive suitable for paper
- scrap paper 4 inches (10.2 cm) square
- black-and-white photocopies of photographs
- craft chalks
- cotton swabs
- scrap card stock in assorted colors (optional)
- ink pads in assorted colors
- craft glue or epoxy
- bamboo pattern on page 101
- stencil plastic
- gold ink
- craft wire, 18 gauge
- wooden dowel, 1/4-inch (6 mm) diameter, 18 inches (45.7 cm) long
- 2 large wood beads
- acrylic paint in black and navy blue
- skeleton leaf
- brad nails
- decorative picture mounts (optional)

INSTRUCTIONS

1 Measure, mark, and cut 12 pieces of the exotic or handmade paper, each measuring 5 1/2 inches (14 cm) square. Cut twelve more pieces, each 3 1/2 inches (8.9 cm) square.

2 Cover the mat board squares with the larger pieces of paper, wrapping excess paper to the back of each piece and trimming the corners before folding so the edges are mitered on the back. These are the tiles you'll use to build the wall hanging.

3 Cover the back of each piece with the smaller squares, gluing them in place. Mark the top edge of each square on the back to help keep them oriented in the same direction as you work.

4 Fold the scrap paper into fourths. Mark a spot at the loose corner (the one with no folds), placing it 1/8 inch (3 mm) in from the top and side of the paper. Use the punch and hammer to make a hole at this point. Unfold the paper. Mark the top edge of this template as you did the tiles.

5 Use the punch and the template created in step 4 to make holes in the corners of all 12 tiles. Make sure the template and each tile are oriented the same way. Even if the tiles aren't perfectly symmetrical, they will

hang better when assembled if the holes match.

6 Spread out the tiles on your work surface and arrange them in four rows of three.

7 Using the cotton swabs and craft chalks, lightly tint the photocopies of the photographs.

8 Tear or cut the images to the desired size. Mount them onto scraps of the card stock, if desired, or glue the photographs directly to some of the tiles.

9 Use the stamps and assorted ink pads to create images on other tiles. Glue the skeleton leaf to one tile.

10 Follow steps 2 through 4 on page 59 to create a stencil of the bamboo pattern. Place the stencil on one tile and use a cotton swab and gold ink to transfer the image. Remove the stencil and let dry.

11 Wrap the craft wire snugly around the larger wooden dowel, keeping the wraps close together. Make at least 42 wraps.

12 Slide the wire coil off the dowel. Use the wire cutters to cut the coil apart, creating wire loops, i.e., your own homemade jump rings.

13 Paint the smaller wooden dowel and the wooden

beads with one coat of black paint, followed by a light coat of dark blue.

14 Connect the tiles with the jump rings, as shown in the photo. Open and close each jump ring by twisting the cut edges side to side; never open them by pulling the two ends apart, as this weakens and distorts the ring.

15 Finish the wall hanging with a row of jump rings across the top row of tiles. Slide the small painted dowel through these rings, then glue a wooden bead onto each end of the dowel to secure the wall hanging.

16 Use the brad nails or decorative picture mounts, if desired, to hang the wall hanging on the wall.

TOOLS & SUPPLIES

- scissors
- ruler
- pencil
- commercially made rubber stamps in floral and exotic motifs *
- craft knife
- leather punch
- hammer
- cutting board, magazine, or other work surface
- stipple brushes
- wire cutters
- paintbrush
- * Select stamps that evoke floral and/or Asian motifs

ROYAL DRAGON BENCH

THE MYSTERIOUS AND MARVELLOUS DRAGON IS PRESENT EVERYWHERE IN THE CUL-
TURE AND STORIES OF ANCIENT CHINA. THE BELOVED CREATURE WAS THOUGHT TO
LIVE IN THE SKIES, OCEANS, AND MOUNTAINS, AND EMBODIED STRENGTH, GOOD-
NESS, AND THE POWERS OF NATURE ITSELF. ONLY THE EMPEROR OR EMPRESS HAD
THE PREROGATIVE OF DISPLAYING DRAGONS WITH FIVE CLAWS. IF YOU WISH TO
OBSERVE THIS CUSTOM WHEN DECORATING YOUR BENCH, MODIFY THE DESIGN TO
GIVE YOUR DRAGON FOUR CLAWS.

Designer ● Jane Wilson

1 Put on your safety glasses and cut and miter the lumber as directed, or have your local wood shop do it. Sand the edges and ends of all the boards, progressing from coarse to fine sandpaper. Wipe clean with the tack cloth.

2 Enlarge the dragon pattern on a photocopier to fit the bench back, leaving a margin on each end of the back. Transfer the pattern to the back board by placing the dragon pattern face up on the board and taping it in place. Use the pencil to trace over the pattern; apply some pressure to make a discernible imprint in the painted surface of the wood.

3 Paint the dragon design, following the design in the photograph or your own inspiration! Outline with the glitter paint, adding it to selected areas for emphasis. Carefully paint the rest of the board black, using two or three coats and letting dry between coats.

4 Refer to figure 1 on page 112. Drill four equally spaced holes in the two unmitered 1 x 2 x 10 pieces (which will serve as seat supports). The holes will accomodate nails when you attach the seat supports to the side pieces.

5 Drill four equally spaced holes along both ends of the seat board to accommodate the nails you'll use to attach the seat to the seat supports. Slightly stagger the holes so they won't be directly aligned with those you drilled in the 1 x 2 x 10 pieces.

6 Measure and mark the two end pieces 18 inches (45.7 cm) up from their bottom edges. Make another mark 17¼ inches (44.1 cm) up on both pieces.

7 With an end piece flat on the ground, marked side facing up, lay a 1 x 2 x 10 seat support on top so it's aligned with the 17¼-inch (44.1 cm) mark. Use the 2-inch (5 cm) 6d nails to nail the support to the end piece. Repeat with the other end piece and seat support.

8 With the help of a friend, hold an end piece upright and position the end of the seat board so it rests on top of the seat support. Check that the holes you drilled in the seat board aren't directly above the nails holding the seat support to the end piece. Place a scrap piece of 1 x 2 under the support strip to brace it, then use 2-inch (5 cm) nails to nail the seat board to the support piece. Repeat with the other end piece.

9 Predrill four equally spaced holes on both ends of the painted back board, which you'll now attach to the bench assembly. Refer to figure 2 on page 112. Butt the back board up to the upright, rear edges of the 2 x 12 x 24 end pieces, lapping the bottom edge of the back board over the rear edge of the seat board. Use the 2-inch (5 cm) nails (working through the predrilled holes) to nail both ends of the back board to the backs of the end pieces. Use the 1½-inch (3.8 cm) finishing nails (but no

MATERIALS

- lumber cut to following dimensions:
    - 1 piece 1 x 12, 48 inches (121.9 cm) long (to form the back)
    - 1 piece 1 x 12, 45 inches (114.3 cm) long (to form the seat)
    - 2 pieces 2 x 12, each 24 inches (61 cm) long (to form the ends)
    - 2 pieces 1 x 2, each 10 inches (25.4 cm) long, cut with a 45° miter on each end
    - 2 pieces 1 x 2, each 10 inches (25.4 cm) long
- dragon pattern on page 112
- gloss enamel paint, black
- acrylic paints in gold, blue, green, and red
- glitter paint in gold
- 6d finishing nails, 2 inches (5 cm) long
- 4d common nails, 1½ inches (3.8 cm)
- finishing nails, 1½ inches (3.8 cm) long
- polyurethane (optional)

TOOLS & SUPPLIES

- safety glasses
- tape measure
- miter box (optional)
- saw
- sandpaper in assorted grits
- tack cloth
- masking tape
- pencil
- paintbrush
- power drill with 3/32-inch (2.4 mm) drill bit
- hammer
- helpful friend

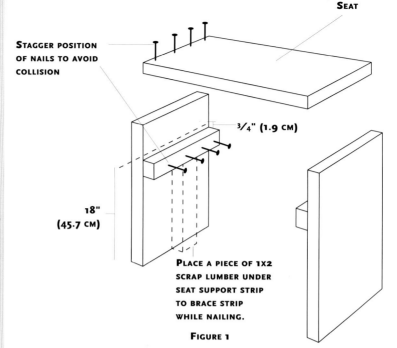

SEAT

STAGGER POSITION OF NAILS TO AVOID COLLISION

3/4" (1.9 CM)

18" (45.7 CM)

PLACE A PIECE OF 1X2 SCRAP LUMBER UNDER SEAT SUPPORT STRIP TO BRACE STRIP WHILE NAILING.

FIGURE 1

predrilled holes) to secure the bottom edge of the back piece to the seat board.

10 If they're not already mitered, cut 45° miters on both ends of the two remaining 1 x 2 x 10 pieces. Install the mitered seat supports 2 inches (5 cm) in from the back edge of the bench,

nailing them in place with the 1½-inch (3.8 cm) finish nails, as shown in figure 2.

11 Paint the unpainted parts of the bench black, using multiple coats for a glossy, finished look.

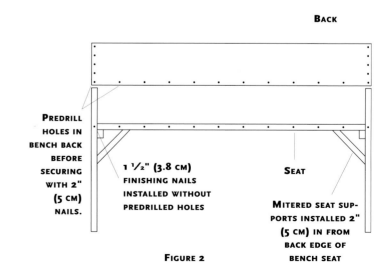

BACK

PREDRILL HOLES IN BENCH BACK BEFORE SECURING WITH 2" (5 CM) NAILS.

1 ½" (3.8 CM) FINISHING NAILS INSTALLED WITHOUT PREDRILLED HOLES

SEAT

MITERED SEAT SUPPORTS INSTALLED 2" (5 CM) IN FROM BACK EDGE OF BENCH SEAT

FIGURE 2

DOUBLE HAPPINESS SCREEN

FENG SHUI TELLS US TO USE SCREENS TO SLOW DOWN CHI AND BLOCK CUTTING ENERGY, BUT THE ANGLES FORMED BY AN UPRIGHT, MULTIPANELED SCREEN MAY CREATE THEIR OWN POISON ARROWS! THIS GORGEOUS SCREEN IS DESIGNED TO AVOID THAT PROBLEM. IT'S DECORATED WITH A GRAPHIC RENDERING OF THE DOUBLE HAPPINESS IDEOGRAM, WHICH INCREASES FAMILY AND MARITAL HARMONY WHEN DISPLAYED IN THE LIVING ROOM OR BEDROOM. IF YOU'D RATHER RESERVE YOUR CREATIVE ENERGIES FOR DECORATING THE SCREEN, HAVE A LOCAL WOOD SHOP CUT THE FRAME PIECES FOR YOU.

Designer ● Cathy Smith

MATERIALS

- **lumber per following specifications:**
  - **4 pieces 1 x 2 x 8**
  - **4 pieces 2 x 2 x 8**
  - **1 piece 2 x 6 x 8**
  - **2 pieces of 2-inch (5 cm) sequential wood strips, each 8 feet (2.4 m) long**＊
- **roll of fiberglass window screen, 4 x 6 feet (m)**
- **8 sheets of decorative, acid-free paper, medium to heavy weight, each 24 x 36 inches (61 x 91.4 cm)**＊＊
- **2 sheets of patterned paper with a ■ reversible, solid side**
- **Double Happiness pattern on page 118**

＊ **Used in the construction of corrugated fiberglass roofing**

＊＊ **Four sheets of translucent cream paper and 4 sheets of colored swirl paper were used in the screen shown in the photo**

TOOLS & SUPPLIES

- **router with 5/8-inch (1.6 cm) routing bit**
- **corner vise**
- **miter box and saw**
- **saw (hand, circular, or table)**
- **carpenter's glue**
- **heavy-duty stapler with 1/4-inch (6 mm) staples**
- **helpful friend**
- **power drill with 1/8- and 1/4-inch (3 and 6 mm) bits**

CONTINUED ON PAGE 115

CONSTRUCTING THE SCREEN FRAMES

1 Refer to figure 1. The frame for the screen is built much like two picture frames, with one picture frame sized to fit inside the other one. First, you'll build the 4 x 6-foot (1.2 x 1.8 m) frame. Measure and mark the 2 x 2s, as shown in figure 2: two 48-inch (121.9 cm) strips and two 72-inch (182.8 cm) strips. Miter cut the ends at 45° angles.

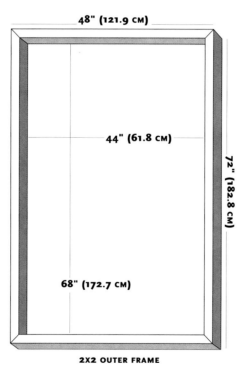

48" (121.9 CM)

44" (61.8 CM)

72" (182.8 CM)

68" (172.7 CM)

2X2 OUTER FRAME

FIGURE 1

2 Place one 6-foot (1.8 m) and one 4-foot (1.2 m) piece in the corner vise. Apply the carpenter's glue to the inner face of their mitered corners, butt the corners together, and secure the vise. Let the glue set. Repeat with the other two pieces.

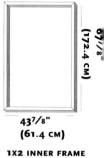

6 7/8" (172.4 CM)

43 7/8" (61.4 CM)

1X2 INNER FRAME

3 Using the 1/8-inch (3 mm) bit, predrill nail holes: two holes in the short leg 1 inch (2.5 cm) in from the corner and 1/2 inch (1.3 cm) from the top and bottom (fig. 3). Drill one hole into the long leg 1 inch in from the corner and 1 inch down from the top. Nail the corners, using the 6d finishing nails, then use the nail set to sink the nail heads a little below the wood's surface. (Do the same when joining the two frame halves together.)

4 Now you'll build the second frame from the 1 x 2 pieces, fitting it inside the 2 x 2 frame. The 2-inch (5 cm)

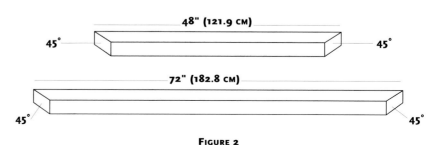

48" (121.9 CM)

45°   45°

72" (182.8 CM)

45°   45°

FIGURE 2

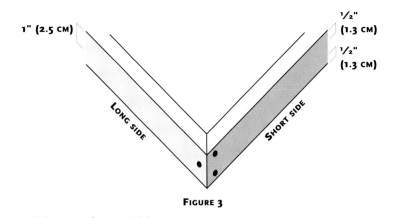

FIGURE 3

side of the 1 x 2 frame will butt up against, and be level with, the inside of the 2 x 2 frame. Measure the inside dimensions of the 2 x 2 frame. Mark the 1 x 2 on its 2-inch side to fit inside the 2 x 2 frame, and use the miter saw to cut a 45° angle on each end of the 1 x 2 (fig. 4). Make sure the cut pieces fit properly before repeating steps 1 through 3 to assemble the second frame.

5 Now you'll cover the front of the 2 x 2 frame with the sequential strips. Measure the front surfaces of the 2 x 2 frame, and cut the sequential strips to the same lengths, mitering the corners. Check the fit of the strips, matching their peaks and valleys in the corners.

6 Run a bead of glue down a leg of the frame and center the matching sequential strip on the leg. Starting at a corner and nailing at 12-inch (cm) intervals, use the 1-¹/₂-inch (3.8 cm) finishing nails to secure the strip. Sink the nail heads. Cover all four legs with strips.

7 Use the wood putty to fill all nail holes and gaps. Let dry. Sand the frames until they're very smooth.

8 Coat both frames with the primer. Let dry and lightly sand. Apply a coat of the black paint, let dry, and lightly sand. Clean well and apply another coat of paint. Let dry, then use the steel wool to gently buff all surfaces. Use the paint thinner and paper towels to clean up.

MAKING THE LEGS

1 Cut the 2 x 6 x 8 in half, making two 4-foot (121.9 cm) lengths. Cut each 4-foot (1.2 m) board (fig. 5 on page 116) so each leg measures

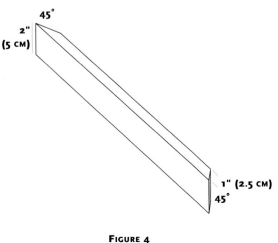

FIGURE 4

CONTINUED FROM PAGE 114

- hammer
- nail set
- scissors
- pencil
- tape measure
- 2 disposable paintbrushes, 1 and 2 inches (2.5 and 5 cm) in width
- wood primer
- 1 quart (0.95 L) oil-based black gloss paint
- 1 pint (0.47 L) glossy polyurethane
- paint thinner
- paper towels
- sandpaper in medium and fine grits
- 2 quarts (1.9 L) flat acrylic decoupage medium
- 6d finishing nails
- 1¹/₂-inch (3.8 cm) finishing nails
- wood filler
- wood screws, 1¹/₂ inches (3.8 cm)
- 2 wood screws, 2¹/₂ inches (6.4 cm)
- 4¹/₄-inch (6 mm) carriage bolts, 3¹/₂ inches (8.9 cm) long
- 4 washers and wing nuts to fit carriage bolts
- fine steel wool
- sheets of newspaper
- white craft glue
- clean rags

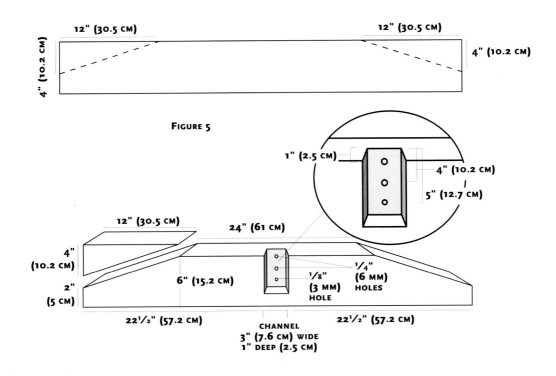

FIGURE 5

FIGURE 6

4 feet at the bottom and 2 feet (61 cm) at the top. Rout a continuous channel, 3 inches (7.6 cm) wide and 1 inch (2.5 cm) deep, across the full 6-inch (15.2 cm) width of the board (fig. 6).

2 Drill holes in the center of the channel, their diameters and spacing, as shown in figure 6. Repeat with the second leg. Prime and paint the legs as you did for the frame (steps 7 and 8 on page 115), leaving only the channel unfinished.

PUTTING THE SCREENING ON THE 1 X 2 FRAME

1 Refer to figure 7 to staple the screen to the outer edge of the frame. Stretch the screen gently, giving it just enough tension to prevent ripples. Center the screen-ing on the frame and staple it to the center of each leg, always working opposite the last staple.

2 After stapling the screening to the center and leg corners, you can staple a whole section, stapling at 2-inch (5 cm) intervals between center and corner, then go to diagonally opposite sections and staple until finished.

JOINING THE FRAMES

1 Be careful not to scratch the paint when joining the frames. Lay the 1 x 2 frame on a flat surface, screen face up.

2 With a friend's help, center the 2 x 2 frame (sequential strips facing up) over the 1 x 2 frame and gently slide it down and over the frame below.

3 Make sure the frame backs are level with each other. Refer to figure 8. Predrill $\frac{1}{8}$-inch (3 mm) holes for screws in the center of each leg, drilling through the inner frame and into the outer 2 x 2 frame. Don't penetrate the outer surface of the 2 x 2 frame; set your drill bit at $1\frac{1}{2}$ inches (3.8 cm) to prevent this. Sink the $1\frac{1}{2}$-inch wood screws in the holes, making sure they're flush with the wood surface.

4 Drill the corners and sink two screws into each corner, about 2 inches (5 cm) deep, making sure the backs of the frames are flush. Drill and sink two more screws in each long leg, centered on either side of the middle screw and between the middle and corner screws.

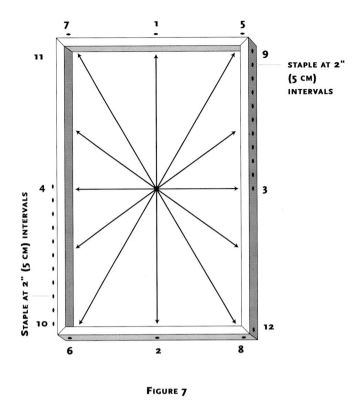

STAPLE AT 2"
(5 CM)
INTERVALS

STAPLE AT 2" (5 CM) INTERVALS

FIGURE 7

5 Paint the screw heads black and let dry. Paint the frames and legs with two coats of the polyurethane. Let dry and buff with the steel wool between coats. Apply a final coat of polyurethane and let dry.

6 See figure 9 on page 118. Stand the frame upright and slide the channel of one leg onto the frame. Make sure the bottoms of the frame and leg are flush and that the frame is perpendicular to the ground. Using the predrilled holes as a guide, continue drilling the $1/4$-inch (6 mm) holes all the way through the frame. Drill the $1/8$-inch (3 mm) hole only 2 inches (5 cm) into the frame—not all the way through. Repeat for the second leg. Install the carriage bolts and screws.

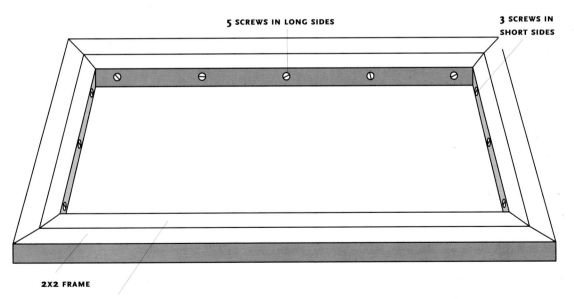

5 SCREWS IN LONG SIDES

3 SCREWS IN SHORT SIDES

2X2 FRAME

1X2 FRAME

FIGURE 8

1 Remove the bolts, screws, and legs, and lay the screen flat on top of layers of newspaper, its front side up.

2 Trim the four sheets of cream paper so they cover the interior of the frame and overlap ½-inch (1.3 cm) in the center.

3 Using the decoupage medium, glue the paper sheets to the surface of the screen. Starting in a corner and working outward, use the 3-inch (7.6 cm) brush to apply the medium to the screen in 1-foot-square (30.5 cm) sections, smoothing on the paper and adhering the next section until the entire sheet is affixed. Repeat with the three remaining sheets. Let dry.

4 Flip the screen over and repeat steps 2 and 3 to apply the colored papers. Let dry.

APPLYING THE PAPER TRIM AND
THE DOUBLE HAPPINESS
SYMBOL

1 Use the scissors to cut the 24 x 36-inch (61 x 91.4 cm) paper lengthwise into a total of seven strips 4 inches (10.2 cm) wide. Reserve the leftover paper.

2 Place a paper strip patterned side up and fold a ½-inch (1.3 cm) edge lengthwise. Fold up the edge again to create a doubled, ½-inch strip with the contrasting color of the reverse side showing along the bottom of the paper strip (the black, decorative trim you see

framing the screen in the photo). Using the craft glue, glue the folded edge. Repeat with the remaining strips. Lay the strips along the edges of the screen.

3 Using the scissors, miter the strips that meet at the corners, cutting the ends into a 45° angle. Butt the mitered corners overlapping them ⅛ inch (3 mm). Use the decoupage medium to glue them down. Let dry.

4 Enlarge the Double Happiness symbol to a diameter of 17 inches (43.2 cm). Trace it onto the reverse side of the leftover border paper and cut it out with scissors. Use the medium to glue it about two-thirds of the way up from the bottom of the screen. Let dry.

5 Use the medium to seal and protect the paper, working from the center to the edges to cover the entire surface, front, and back of the paper. Let one side dry before sealing the other.

6 Clean the screen with a rag dampened with water (no solvents or cleaning agents). Reassemble the screen.

LEG	2X2 FRAME	1X2 FRAME

NOT TO SCALE

FIGURE 9

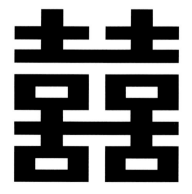

DOUBLE HAPPINESS PATTERN

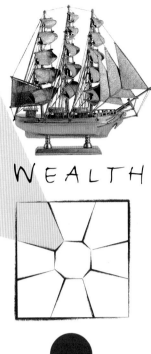

WEALTH

ELEMENT ▪ WOOD

I CHING ▪ TRIGRAM WIND

COMPASS DIRECTION ▪ SOUTHEAST

MOVEMENT OF CHI ▪ UPWARD

SHAPES ▪ NO FIXED FORM

COLORS ▪ PURPLES, BLUES, REDS, GREENS

MATERIALS ▪ SHIMMERING, RICH TEXTURES, THINGS THAT MOVE, EXPENSIVE ITEMS

IMAGERY ▪ MONEY, SAILING SHIPS, ENRICHING OR POSITIVE IMAGERY (ANY SYMBOLISM IN WEALTH, FOR GOOD OR BAD, HAS GREAT POWER)

If there is one sector of the bagua where you should spare no expense, Wealth is it! Also called Intention or Empowerment, this very powerful sector draws the attention and supportive energies of the universe to you. Everything you place here should be sparkling clean, perfectly maintained, and as costly, beautiful, and/or luxurious as you can afford. Large, lush plants, wind chimes, crystals, and aquariums or fountains are also helpful. Erect screens or hang sheers over any large windows in this area to keep chi from escaping. Note that mirrors also function as windows—where chi might leak out—and should be kept to a minimum here.

CRYSTAL AND VELVET TABLE RUNNER

SUMPTUOUS VELVET AND CRYSTAL BEADS ARE PERFECT MATERIALS FOR THE WEALTH SECTOR OF THE BAGUA. THIS BEAUTIFUL TABLE RUNNER IS STENCILED WITH SUBTLE IMAGES OF COINS, AND COINS TIED TO BOTH ENDS ATTRACT PROSPERITY, TOO.

Designer ● *Lynn Krucke*

1 Spread out the velvet on your work surface, plush side up, and insert pins to mark the desired locations for the rubber stamp image.

2 With the stamp position wood side down on a firm surface, turn over the velvet and place the plush surface against the rubber side of the stamp at the first pin. When everything is positioned to your satisfaction, remove the pin.

3 Heat the iron (on dry setting, no steam). Spritz the back of the velvet lightly with the water. Place the hot iron on top of the velvet and hold for about 15 seconds. The plush surface of the velvet will be permanently flattened, transferring the image on the stamp to the velvet.

4 Lift the iron and allow the velvet to cool. Leaving the stamp on the worktable, find another pinned spot on the velvet and place it over the stamp.

5 Repeat steps 3 and 4, removing pins as you work, until all marked areas have been ironed.

6 Cut the lining fabric to the same size as the velvet.

7 Pin together the lining and velvet, right sides together. Fold the assembly in half lengthwise and cut each end to a point.

8 Using a 5/8-inch (1.6 cm) seam, sew around the edges of the runner. Leave a 4-inch (10.2 cm) opening unsewn along one side.

9 Remove the pins and turn the runner right side out. Slipstitch the 4-inch (10.2 cm) opening closed by hand.

10 With the lining side up, use the iron and gently press along the edges to flatten the seams, being very careful not to damage the nap of the velvet.

11 Sew one bead and one charm to each pointed end of the runner. Tie the threads securely before trimming.

TOOLS & MATERIALS

- 1/3 yard (30.5 cm) rayon/acetate velvet, 45 inches (114.3 cm) wide
- straight pins
- commercially produced rubber stamp in image of Chinese coin
- spritzer bottle filled with water
- iron
- 1/3 yard (30.5 cm) cotton fabric for lining, 45 inches (114.3 cm) wide
- scissors
- thread to match fabric
- sewing machine
- 2 faceted glass beads
- 2 charms in shape of Chinese coins✳
- sewing needle

✳ **Available in bead stores**

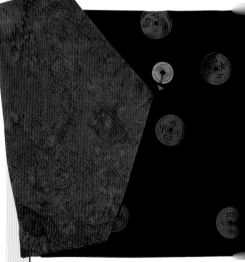

DRAGON FAN LAMP

THIS BEAUTIFUL AND INVENTIVE LAMP IS A WONDERFUL WAY TO BRING MORE FIRE ELEMENT AND YANG ENERGY INTO YOUR HOME. IT FEATURES FENG SHUI'S MOST POWERFUL CELESTIAL CREATURE: THE DRAGON, SYMBOL OF LUCK, STRENGTH, WISDOM, AND PROTECTION. THE SHADE IS CRAFTED FROM READY-MADE FANS, WHICH SYMBOLICALLY DISPEL NEGATIVE ENERGIES.

Designer

●

Jean Tomaso Moore

1 Use the hacksaw to saw off the center prongs on the plant basket, as shown in figure 1. Use the file to smooth any jagged metal.

2 Unscrew the plastic cap that holds the metal shade to the lamp, remove shade, and place the wire plant basket onto the bulb opening to check for fit. Screw the plastic cap onto the bulb opening to test the stability and fit of the shade, as shown in figure 2. Remove the basket, retaining the cap.

FIGURE 2

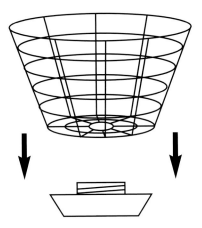

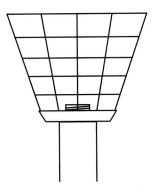

FIGURE 1

3 Use the craft paper to make a template of the outside of the basket by wrapping it around the basket, making sure the ends of the craft paper overlap. Mark the upper and lower edges of the basket, then cut out the template.

4 On a flat surface, lay the template on top of the red paper. Draw around the edge of the template, then cut out the pattern from the red paper.

5 Working outside for ventilation, use the spray adhesive to adhere the red paper cutout to the outside of the basket.

- 16-inch (40.6 cm) wire plant basket
- black metal torchère-style floor lamp with metal shade*
- brown craft paper
- 2 sheets red, transparent, hand-made paper, 25 x 30 inches (63.5 x 76.2 cm) each
- spray adhesive
- 4 red fans, 18-inch (45.7 cm) diameter, printed with dragon design
- 1-inch (2.5 cm) masking tape
- black acrylic craft paint, 2 ounces (28 gm)
- decorative tassel (optional)

*You can find inexpensive models in home improvement stores.

TOOLS & SUPPLIES

- hacksaw
- metal file
- pencil
- scissors
- flat-head screw driver
- hot glue gun and glue sticks
- paintbrush or foam brush

6 Adjust the paper template to fit the inside of the basket. Repeat step 4, using the second sheet of red paper, then trim the red cutout to fit inside the planter. Use spray adhesive to adhere it to the inside of the basket.

7 Now you'll prepare the fans. Use the screwdriver to pop the rivets off of the bottoms of the fans and spread the fans out on a flat work surface.

8 Hot glue the fans together at their seams (the end ribs) as shown in figure 3.

9 Lay two strips of masking tape across all the fan ribs, making the tape as symmetrical as possible and adhering the tape to both sides of the fans.

10 Use the black acrylic paint to paint the tape strips on both sides. Let dry.

11 Wrap the fan assembly around the paper-covered basket frame, cutting off any overlap. Use hot glue to adhere the fans to the frame.

12 Place the shade on the lamp. Replace the plastic cap and screw into place. Hang a decorative tassel from the on/off switch if desired.

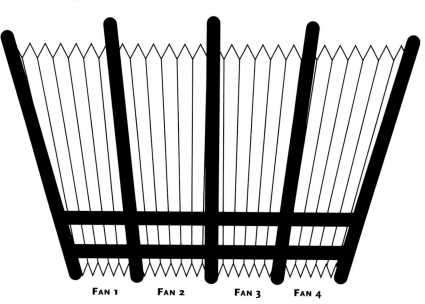

FAN 1   **FAN 2**   **FAN 3**   **FAN 4**

FIGURE 3

MESH PILLAR CANDLE

THE YANG ENERGY OF CANDLES IS HIGHLY RECOMMENDED FOR THE **W**EALTH SECTOR OF THE BAGUA, AND THE EMBELLISHMENTS OF SHIM-MERING METAL AND COINS ALSO ATTRACT AUSPICIOUS CHI AND PROS-PERITY. **A**S THE CANDLE BURNS, ROLL DOWN THE WIRE MESH COVERING.

Designer

●

Terry Taylor

TOOLS & MATERIALS

- **pillar candle in rich red, blue, green, or purple**
- **newspaper**
- **scissors**
- **copper or brass screen wire***
- **hole punch**
- **hot glue gun and glue sticks**
- **thin-gauge copper wire**
- **power drill (optional)**
- **Chinese "coin" look-alikes*****
- **vise (optional)**

***Available in craft stores**

*****Usually stocked by bead stores**

INSTRUCTIONS

1 Wrap the newspaper around the pillar candle, overlapping the ends 1/2 inch (1.3 cm). Use the scissors to cut away excess length.

2 Create a template by trimming the newspaper rectangle to the same height as the candle.

3 Lay the template over the screen wire and cut out a rectangle.

4 Use the hole punch to make holes along the top and bottom edges of the screen wire rectangle.

5 Wrap the wire rectangle around the candle. Use a small amount of hot glue about halfway up the height of the candle to hold the rectangle in place.

6 Cut lengths of the copper wire 3 to 4 inches (7.6 to 10.2 cm) longer than the circumference of the candle. Twist the wires together: Secure several strands in the chuck of a drill, secure the other ends of the wires in a vise, and rotate the drill to twist the wires together.

ABUNDANCE FRUIT BASKETS

DISPLAYING A BOWL OF LUSCIOUS FRUIT IS ONE WAY TO ATTRACT PROSPERITY TO YOUR HOME, AND THE QUIET LUXURY OF THESE STUNNING BASKETS MAKES THEM PERFECT FOR THE WEALTH GUA.

Designer ● Terry Taylor

1 To create an 8-inch-square (20.3 cm) basket, use the pencil and ruler to measure an 8-inch square on the paper and cut it out. Modify the measurement if you'd like a basket of a different size.

2 Press the length of hardware cloth flat, then center the paper pattern on top. Tape it down.

3 Now you'll cut away four corners from the hardware cloth square to create a cross shape. Cut one section at a time with the wire cutters, starting the cut from the edge of the cloth and working to an outer corner of the paper square. Rotate the hardware cloth 90° and make an equivalent cut to the same corner. Repeat with the other three corners.

4 Use the wire cutters to remove the sharp stickers on the edges of the hardware cloth.

5 Using the scrap of 2 x 4 lumber as an edge, gently folding the basket's side up, one at a time. To adjust their height, place the dowel along the top edge of a side and gently roll down the edge. Estimate how much cloth is needed to make the rolled edge, add it to the desired height of the sides, and cut off any excess. Don't roll the edge yet.

6 Using the wire cutters, cut a length of the steel wire twice as long as the height of the basket sides.

7 Wire together the sides two at a time, using the twist ties or bulldog clips to hold them together while you work. Starting at the bottom of the basket, join the two sides with a 1/2-inch (1.3 cm) length of wire twisted onto the longer length of wire you cut earlier. Use the needle-nose pliers to twist the wire tightly but not too tightly, or you'll break the hardware cloth.

8 Using the wire like thread, make a whipstitch up the side. Stitch every square and tighten the stitch with the pliers as you go along. Don't let the stitching wire kink. Whipstitch to the desired height and leave the end of the wire free. Repeat with the other sides.

9 Roll the top of the side outward around the dowel, pressing gently so it keeps its shape. Use a twist tie to secure each end to the side of the basket at this point.

10 Use the free end of the (stitching) wire to whipstitch the rolled edge. Wrap around the wire a couple of times and snip it off with the cutters. Finish the rest of the edges the same way.

11 Use the flat file to remove any burrs on the corners of the basket or the ends of the rolled edges. Fill the basket with the fruit of your choice.

MATERIALS

- paper
- hardware cloth with a 1/4-inch (6 mm) mesh, 24 inches (61 cm) long
- roll of 22-gauge steel wire

TOOLS & SUPPLIES

- pencil
- ruler
- scissors
- masking tape
- wire cutters or metal shears
- scrap of 2 x 4 lumber, 6 to 8 inches (15.2 to 20.3 cm) long
- wooden dowel, 3/4 to 1 inch (1.9 to 2.5 cm) long
- bulldog clips or twist ties
- needle-nose pliers
- flat file
- fruit (optional)

FAME OR REPUTATION

ELEMENT ■ FIRE
I CHING ■ TRIGRAM FIRE
COMPASS DIRECTION ■ SOUTH
MOVEMENT OF CHI ■ OUTWARD
SHAPES ■ TRIANGLES, POINTED, CONICAL, ZIGZAGS
COLORS ■ REDS, MAROONS
IMAGERY ■ SUNS, STARS, PYRAMIDS, TRIANGLES

Seeing red is not always a bad thing, especially in the Fame sector of the bagua. Some feng shui practitioners think it's impossible to add too much of that color to this area if you want to enhance your reputation and public recognition of your work. Use darker hues such as maroon or rose if they better suit your taste. Add awards or prizes you've received, animal materials or figures which symbolize life's fire, candles, and fire-shape objects. If you're lucky, you may even have a fireplace in this sector. Avoid any kind of Water, real or symbolic. If a Water element room, such as a bathroom, is located in this sector of your house, redecorate—and make it red!

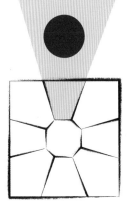

COPPER PYRAMID LAMP

THIS LAMP CAPTURES THE ESSENCE OF THE FIRE ELEMENT WITH ITS POINTED PROFILE, GENTLY GLOWING PIERCINGS AND GEMS, AND BEAUTIFULLY PATINATED COPPER. IT'S ALSO EMBELLISHED WITH A GRAPHIC INTERPRETATION OF THE FIRE IDEOGRAM.

Designer

●

Cathy Smith

INSTRUCTIONS

CREATING THE LAMP PIECES

1 Refer to figure 1. Put on the safety glasses and gloves. Always wear them when working with metal; cut edges are very sharp. Measure and mark four identical triangles as shown. Their bases should measure 9 inches (22.9 cm), sides 12³/₄ inches (32.4 cm), and height 12 inches (30.5 cm). Use the metal shears to cut them out, then clip off ¹/₄ inch (6 mm) of the topmost point of each triangle, blunting it.

2 Place the board on a sturdy worktable, lay a copper triangle on top with its left edge hanging over the board by ¹/₄ inch (6 mm), and clamp them to the table.

3 Using the rubber mallet, bend down the overhanging edge of the copper so it forms a right angle to the triangle.

4 Photocopy the template in figure 2 on page 132, enlarging as noted. This will serve as your punch pattern. Cut away the excess margin, then tape the template to the triangle, using the tacks to secure the bottom and right sides (fig. 3) to prevent the copper from curling while you punch it.

5 Use the awl and hammer to practice punching holes in scrap sheet, then punch all holes in the template. Next, use the nail set and hammer to enlarge the holes where indicated. If desired, you may choose to put the Fire symbol on one side only.

6 Repeat steps 2 through 5 for the remaining three sides.

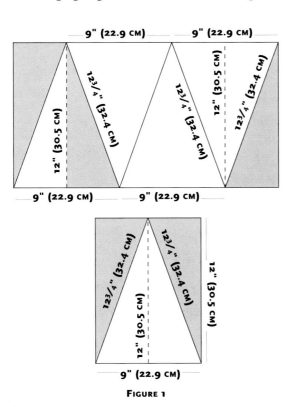

FIGURE 1

CONTINUED ON PAGE 132

MATERIALS

- **thin-gauge copper sheet, in a 12 x 23-inch (cm) sheet or precut into four 9 x 12-inch (30.5 cm) triangles**
- **template on page 132**
- **copper patina antiquing solution**
- **small paintbrush**
- **glass jewels in green and orange**
- **3 feet (0.9 m) of vinyl minitubing, ¹/₄-inch (6 mm) diameter***
- **prewired lamp base, no more than 4 inches (10.2 cm) high**
- **25- to 40-watt lightbulb**
- *** Found in aquarium supply stores**

TOOLS & SUPPLIES

- **safety glasses**
- **work gloves**
- **ruler**
- **pencil or black fine-tip permanent marker**
- **metal shears**
- **scrap piece of 2 x 4 lumber**
- **C-clamps**
- **rubber mallet**
- **masking tape**
- **thumb or upholstery tacks**
- **awl**
- **small hammer**
- **nail set**
- **propane soldering torch (optional)***

- **clear plumber's adhesive**
- **vise or vise grip pliers**
- **fine steel wool**
- **small paintbrush**
- **small, sharp scissors**
- ✽ **Found in plumbing departments of home improvement stores**

PUNCH PATTERN TEMPLATE

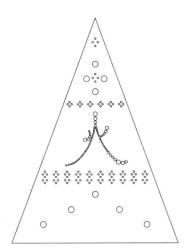

FIGURE 2

Enlarge 200%, then another 200%, then 125%.

7 If desired, use the soldering torch to discolor the copper by lightly passing it over the material in selected places. Be careful to do this in a safe environment, away from flammable materials. Take care not to use too much heat or you'll weaken the metal.

ASSEMBLING AND DECORATING THE LAMP

1 Run a bead of the adhesive along the inner edge of the $1/4$-inch (6 mm) flap on a triangle and join it to the right side of a second triangle. Use the vise or vise grip pliers to support the join while the glue sets. Join only two sides at a time and let cure before proceeding. Run a smooth line of adhesive along the inner seam of the joint and let cure again. Avoid getting adhesive in the punch holes. Continue until you've formed a pyramid shape.

2 Using the rubber mallet, gently hammer out any irregularities along the outer seams and apex of the pyramid.

3 Using the steel wool, scour the surface of the metal to clean it. Use the small paintbrush to apply the antiquing solution, one face of the pyramid at a time, allowing the solution to dry before the next application.

4 Use the adhesive to adhere the glass jewels.

5 Use the metal shears to cut a $1/2$-inch (1.3 cm) semicircle from the bottom of one panel of the pyramid to accommodate the electrical cord of the lighting fixture.

6 Now you'll finish the bottom of the pyramid so it won't mar your tabletop. Using the small scissors, make a slit along one side of the entire length of vinyl tubing.

7 Run a light bead of the adhesive along the inside, bottom edge of the pyramid, then slip the tubing over the edge. Manipulate the tubing so it follows the semicircle you cut in the base as well. Join the ends of the tubing, cutting off any excess. Let dry.

8 Screw the bulb into the lamp base and set the pyramid on top, feeding the electrical cord out of the semicircle you cut out in step 5.

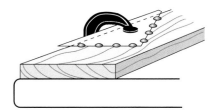

FIGURE 3

Embossed Pyramid Candles

These candles are perfect additions to the **Fame** or **Fire** sector of a room. The symbolic yang energy of animal motifs and other creatures enhances the energetic impact of red candles, and the pyramid shapes represent **Fire** element, too. Because of the decals used to embellish the candles, it's best to burn them only briefly, then use them strictly for decoration.

Designer ● Lynn Krucke

TOOLS & MATERIALS

- **water slide decal paper (made for use with toner-based photocopiers)**
- **antistatic dryer sheet**
- **commercially produced rubber stamps with dragon and butterfly images**
- **pigment ink pad (gold)**
- **gold and silver embossing powders**
- **embossing heat gun**
- **scissors**
- **bowl of water**
- **paper towels or soft cloth**
- **red candles in pyramidal shapes**

INSTRUCTIONS

1 First, decide how many motifs you'd like to apply to a candle. Use the dryer sheet to wipe the shiny side of a piece of the water slide decal paper.

2 Ink a rubber stamp with gold pigment ink and stamp the image firmly onto the shiny side of the water slide decal paper.

3 Before the ink dries, quickly but carefully tap the embossing powder over the stamped image, covering the image. The candles shown in the photo incorporate gold powder on the dragons and silver on the butterflies. Return any excess powder to the container so you can use it again.

4 Use the heat gun to heat the image until the embossing powder melts.

5 Repeat steps 2 through 4 until the desired number of images have been stamped and embossed.

6 Cut out each image, taking care not to cut into the embossed areas.

7 Place a trimmed image in the bowl of water. (It will curl.) Let it soak until the paper backing is thoroughly saturated with water.

8 Remove the image from the bowl and blot it gently on the paper towels or cloth.

9 Carefully slide the paper backing slightly to one side, position the embossed image on the candle, then completely remove the backing paper.

10 Smooth the image in place, pushing out air bubbles and blotting away any drops of water.

11 Repeat steps 7 through 10 with the remaining images.

12 When all the images have been transferred to the candle, use the heat gun to gently and carefully heat each one until the edges of the decal "disappear" into the candle. Be careful and don't overheat it!

TABLETOP VOTIVE LANTERNS

FIRE AND FIERY COLORS ARE PERFECT FOR ENERGIZING THE FAME SECTOR, AND THE IDEOGRAMS ON THESE INVENTIVE VOTIVE CANDLE COVERS TRADITIONALLY ATTRACT PROSPERITY, LONG LIFE, AND LOTS OF GOLD! MAKE ONE OF EACH, OR COVER A TABLETOP WITH THEM.

Designer  *Terry Taylor*

TOOLS & MATERIALS

- **black, single-face, corrugated paper**
- **pencil**
- **metal-edge ruler**
- **craft knife**
- **templates on this page**
- **black fine-point permanent marker**
- **vellum**
- **large and small paper punches**
- **white craft glue**
- **waxed paper**
- **heavy book**
- **brass wire fasteners✢**
- **glass votive candle holders**
- **votive candles**
- **✢Available at office supply stores**

INSTRUCTIONS

1 Measure and mark 6 x 14-inch (15.2 x 35.6 cm) rectangles on the smooth side of the single-face corrugated paper, one per lantern. Use the craft knife to cut them out.

2 Mark a 3 x 4-inch (7.6 x 10.2 cm) rectangle centered on the corrugated paper. Cut it out.

3 Photocopy and enlarge the templates for the Chinese ideograms below. The ideogram in figure 1 is a charm to ensure longevity and prosperity. The ideogram in figure 2 traditionally attracts wealth.

4 Mark 3½ x 4½-inch (8.9 x 11.4 cm) rectangles on the vellum, one per lantern. Cut them out.

5 Place a vellum rectangle on top of one of the characters. Use the permanent marker to trace the character onto the vellum. Then fill in the outlined character until it's solid black. Repeat for as many lanterns as you're creating.

6 Randomly punch large shapes in the corrugated paper rectangles.

7 Punch small holes along the top and bottom edges. The designer used triangular shapes (symbols of fire) along the edges.

8 Cut small pieces of vellum to cover the large punched shapes.

9 Glue the vellum containing the traced ideogram and the small pieces of vellum onto the smooth side of the corrugated paper with the "right side" of the ideogram facing out. Cover with waxed paper, weight it with the book, and let dry overnight.

10 Roll the corrugated paper into a cylinder, overlapping the edges slightly. Use the small hole punch to punch two holes at the top and bottom of the over-lapped edges. Use the brass wire fasteners to hold the cylinder together.

11 Set the completed lantern over a small votive candle in a glass container. Be safe; don't leave a burning candle unattended.

PROSPERITY AND LONG LIFE

ABUNDANT GOLD

RELATIONSHIP OR COMMITMENT

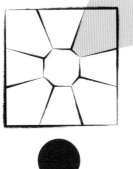

ELEMENT ▪ EARTH

I CHING TRIGRAM ▪ EARTH

COMPASS DIRECTION ▪ SOUTHWEST

MOVEMENT OF CHI ▪ DOWNWARD

SHAPES ▪ NO FIXED FORM

COLORS ▪ PINKS, WHITES, REDS, YELLOWS

MATERIALS ▪ TACTILE, SENSUAL. NO SHARP OR CUTTING EDGES.

**IMAGERY ▪ THINGS IN PAIRS, GROUPS, AND COLLECTIONS.
PHOTOS OF LOVED ONES. ROMANTIC IMAGERY. NO SOLO OBJECTS.**

As you would imagine for the Relationship sector of the bagua, pairs, collections, and groupings of objects belong here. This sector's energies are very feminine, but they affect all partnerships and relationships in your life, not only the romantic. Avoid any imagery or objects representing division or violence. (No scissors. No war memorabilia. Not even a spiky plant! You get the idea.) Stripes symbolize strife, so avoid using them. Decorate this sector with pairs of things, such as two bedside lamps or two hassocks, and avoid any object which implies solo attention, such as a television or computer.

EASY CHINESE HASSOCKS

THIS PAIR OF STRIKING DEMI-HASSOCKS ARE PERFECT FOR FLANKING A BED AND ENERGIZING THE RELATIONSHIPS SECTOR. YOU CAN ADAPT THE MEASUREMENTS OF THE FABRIC COVERS TO FIT HASSOCKS YOU ALREADY HAVE, OR HAVE WOOD CUT AT YOUR LOCAL HOME IMPROVEMENT STORE AND MAKE YOUR OWN EASY-TO-BUILD BENCHES. NO NEED TO PAINT THEM SINCE THE COVERS WILL BE ON TOP!

Designer ● *Jane Wilson*

INSTRUCTIONS

MAKING THE BENCHES

1 To avoid confusion, it's best to construct one bench at a time. Sand the edges and ends of the cut lumber to remove any roughness. Wipe clean with the tack cloth.

2 Using the scrap piece of 1 x 2 lumber as a visual reference to help align the marks, make five evenly spaced marks on both ends of the 1 x 12 x 24-inch (2.5 x 30.5 x 61 cm) seat piece. The marks indicate where holes will be drilled for nails.

3 Use the finish nails to nail the 2 x 12 x 16 1/2-inch (2.5 x 30.5 x 41.9 cm) end pieces underneath the seat (fig. 1).

4 Position the 1 x 2 x 21 1/4 (2.5 x 5 x 56.4 cm) between the ends and under the seat, as shown in figure 1. Use the drill and wood screws to secure as shown.

5 Repeat steps 1 through 4 to construct the second bench.

MAKING THE HASSOCK COVERS

1 Take the pattern to a copy shop and have them produce it as a heat transfer measuring 7 1/2 inches (19 cm) in diameter.

2 Use the scissors to trim excess material around the heat transfer, leaving a 1/8-inch (3 mm) margin.

3 As indicated in figure 2 on page 140, pin the adhesive flags or make chalk marks on the pieces of fabric where notches are indicated to help you match up the pieces when sewing.

4 Make one cover at a time. After trimming excess material to leave only a narrow margin around the heat transfer, center the heat transfer design on the right side of one of the 25 x 52-inch (63.5 x 132 cm) pieces of fabric (fig. 2). Lay the clean cloth over the heat transfer and iron on the transfer.

5 Refer to figure 3 on page 141. Right sides together, pin the

MATERIALS

■ lumber cut to following dimensions*:

  ■ 4 pieces 2 x 12, 16 1/2 inches (41.9 cm) long to form the ends

  ■ 2 pieces 1 x 12, 24 inches (61 cm) long to form the seats

  ■ 4 pieces 1 x 2, 21 1/4 inches (56.4 cm) long to form the supports between the ends

■ scrap piece of 1 x 2 lumber

*Note that 2 x 12, 1 x 12, etc., are industry specifications and actual dimensions will differ. The project directions account for this and do not need to be adjusted.

■ 2 pieces foam, 1 inch (2.5 cm) thick, each 12 x 24 inches (30.5 x 61cm)

■ fabric, 4 pieces measuring 12-1/2 x 20 inches (31.8 x 50.8 cm) each, 2 pieces measuring 25 x 52 inches (63.5 x 132 cm) each

■ pattern on page 59

■ thread to match fabric

■ newspaper

■ black puff paint

■ black microfine glitter

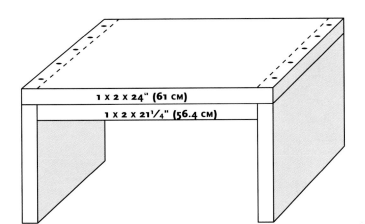

1 X 2 X 24" (61 CM)
1 X 2 X 21 1/4" (56.4 CM)

FIGURE 1

12$\frac{1}{2}$ x 20-inch (31.8 x 50.8 cm) pieces to the large piece, as shown in figure 3, matching notches. Using $\frac{1}{4}$-inch (6 mm) seams, sew them together but stop stitching the seams at the $\frac{1}{4}$-inch seam allowance; this will allow you to use a timesaving technique to create the corners of the hassock covers. Remove the flags and pins.

6 Refer to figure 4. On the long piece of material (not the side pieces), clip the piece at both ends of the stitching, making a cut no longer than $\frac{1}{4}$ inch (6 mm). The

purpose is to create some "give" in the larger piece so you can twist the edge of the larger piece down and around, as shown in figure 3, aligning its edge with the selvage of the side piece, right sides together. Pin the edges together and sew with a $\frac{1}{4}$-inch (6 mm) seam. Repeat to create the other three corners and corner seams of the hassock.

7 Turn in a $\frac{1}{4}$-inch (6 mm) edge along the raw edge of the cover and iron it in place. Measure and turn up a 1$\frac{1}{4}$-inch (3.1 cm) hem

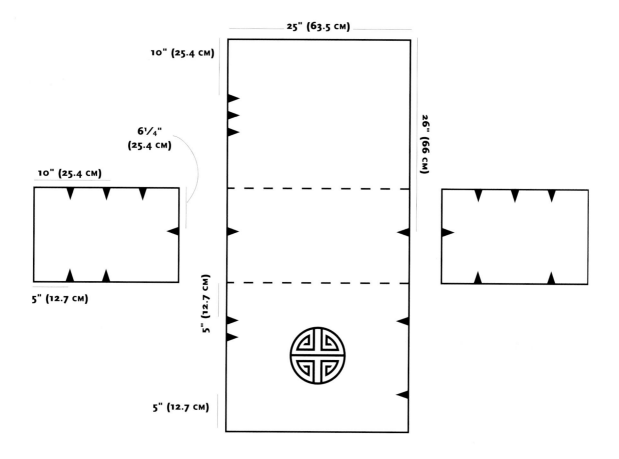

FIGURE 2

and hem in place.

8 Repeat steps 4 through 7 to make the second cover.

9 To give the heat transfer dimension and sparkle, lay the cover flat on a worktable with the motif facing up. Slip several layers of newspaper under the top layer of fabric to prevent bleeding through. Working steadily and slowly, apply a generous line of the black puff paint along all lines of the motif, then quickly sprinkle glitter on the paint before it dries. Repeat with the other cover. Let dry undisturbed overnight. Make sure the paint is dry, then shake off the glitter.

10 Place a piece of foam on top of each bench, and slip the fabric covers over the benches.

TOOLS & SUPPLIES

- sandpaper
- tack cloth
- measuring tape
- pencil
- hammer
- 6d finish nails, 2 inches (5 cm) long
- power drill with 3/32-inch (2.4 mm) drill bit
- wood screws, 1 1/2 inch (3.8 cm)
- scissors
- small adhesive plastic flags*
- straight pins
- sewing machine
- clean cloth
- iron
- newspaper

* Found in office supply stores

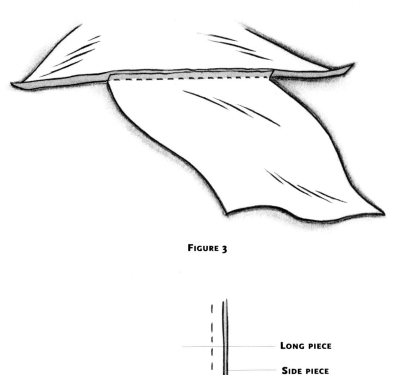

FIGURE 3

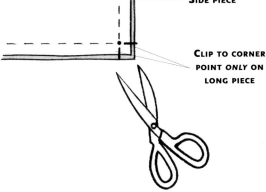

LONG PIECE

SIDE PIECE

CLIP TO CORNER POINT *ONLY* ON LONG PIECE

FIGURE 4

EMBOSSED MANDARIN DUCK BOXES

MANDARIN DUCKS ARE A BELOVED SYMBOL OF YOUNG LOVE TO THE CHINESE, BUT THERE'S NO REASON THEY CAN'T SPEAK TO THE YOUNG AT HEART AS WELL. THEY ARE ALWAYS DISPLAYED AS A PAIR, NEVER SOLO. MAKE ONE BOX FOR YOURSELF AND ONE FOR YOUR SIGNIFICANT OTHER—OR FOR THE NEW LOVE YOU'D LIKE TO INVITE INTO YOUR LIFE.

Designer ● Cathy Smith

1 Refer to figures 1A (below) and 1B (page 144). First, you'll use the bottom and lid of a box as templates to create the foil covering. Lay them on the aluminum sheet and use the fine-point stylus to score around them, flipping them onto their sides as necessary to score each dimension. Measure and mark two $1/4$-inch (6 mm) overlap flaps on the two opposing sides of the bottom and lid, as shown in figure 1, and add a $1/2$-inch (1.3 cm) extension flap as shown; this will fold over the edges of the box and lid to line the interiors. Make score lines where indicated by the dotted lines in figure 1. Repeat to create the foil coverings for the second box and lid.

2 Use the scissors to cut out the foil shapes.

3 Photocopy the patterns on page 145, enlarging as directed. Now you'll begin embossing the lids. Place the foam core on your work surface, then place a foil lid cover on top, face up. Tape a duck pattern in the center of the foil, then tape the foil to the work surface.

4 Use the fine-point stylus to emboss the duck pattern, using short repeated strokes. Repeat the process with the side patterns.

- 2 papier mâché boxes with lids, each 4 inches (10.2 cm) square
- 36-gauge aluminum tooling foil* or disposable aluminum over liner pans
- fine-point stylus with a rounded, $1/16$-inch (1.6 mm) tip, or a dried-up ball point pen
- ruler
- black fine-tip permanent marker
- utility scissors*
- patterns on page 145
- piece of foam board with "give," to use as work surface
- masking tape
- stylus with a rounded, $1/4$-inch (6 mm) tip, or a chopstick
- heavy white craft glue
- poster board or other thin card board
- scraps of decorative fabric to use for box linings
- wooden clothespins with spring hinges
- fine steel wool
- $1/2$-inch (1.3 cm) paintbrush
- dark antiquing solution or wood stain
- paper towels
- * Scissors used to cut metal foil should be reserved for that purpose.

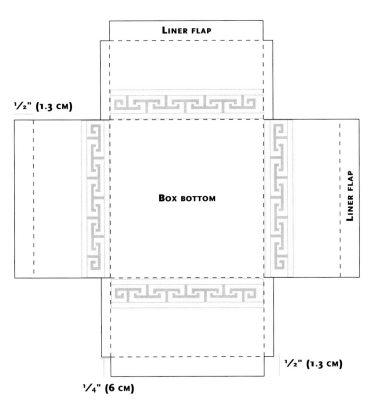

LINER FLAP

$1/2$" (1.3 CM)

LINER FLAP

BOX BOTTOM

$1/2$" (1.3 CM)

$1/4$" (6 CM)

FIGURE 1A

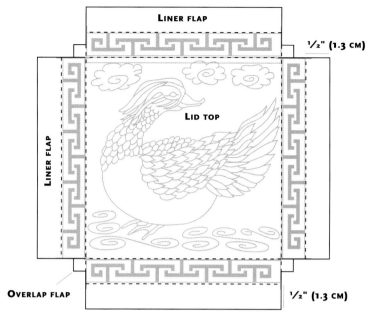

LINER FLAP

LINER FLAP

½" (1.3 CM)

LID TOP

OVERLAP FLAP

½" (1.3 CM)

FIGURE 1B

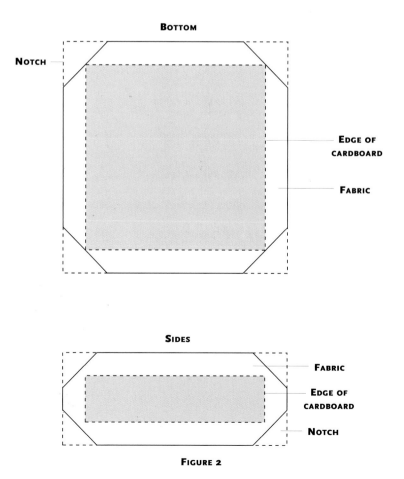

BOTTOM

NOTCH

EDGE OF CARDBOARD

FABRIC

SIDES

FABRIC

EDGE OF CARDBOARD

NOTCH

FIGURE 2

5 Remove the paper pattern and use the fine-point stylus to deepen the outlines. Flip over the foil and use the ¼-inch (6 mm) stylus to give the feathers, tail, and clouds more definition.

6 Repeat steps 3 through 6 to emboss the foil for the second box. Fill the back sides of the embossed pieces with the white glue and let dry overnight to help "crush-proof" the embossing.

7 Lay the foil for the box bottom face down and cover the entire surface with a thin layer of the white glue. Center the box on the foil and fold up the sides, the ¼-inch (6 mm) overlap flaps first, using your fingers to smooth the foil onto the surface. Make sure all scored flaps are folded and adhered inside and

outside the box. Repeat with the other bottom and lids. Let dry.

8 Now you'll line the boxes. Measure the interior sides and bottom of a box, and cut four pieces of the poster board to those dimensions minus 1/8 inch (3 mm). For example, if a side measures 3 3/4 x 1 3/4 inches (9.5 x 4.4 cm), you'll cut the poster board to 3 5/8 x 1 5/8 inches (9.2 x 4.1 cm).

9 Measure the inside of the lid, top only (interior sides are

already foil-covered) and create a matching poster board piece.

10 Use the poster board pieces to cut out pieces of material, adding an extra 1/2 inch (1.3 cm) per side. Notch the corners of the material (fig. 2).

11 Run a light bead of the craft glue around the edges and inner surface of the poster board, then smooth fabric over it. Flip over the piece, add glue around the edges, and fold over the edges of fabric. Repeat, covering all the pieces.

12 When the lining pieces are dry, glue them inside the boxes and lids, using the clothespins to clamp them in place until they dry.

13 Clean off any excess glue on the box surfaces, and use the steel wool to buff the foil.

14 Paint the stain on the embossed surfaces, letting it settle into the outlines and depressions. Use the paper towels to remove excess stain from raised areas and let dry. Stain on metal dries slowly; allow about 72 hours.

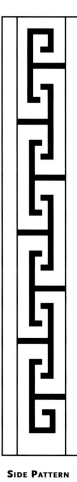

SIDE PATTERN

MANDARIN DUCK BOXES
LID PATTERNS

CHILDREN AND CREATIVITY

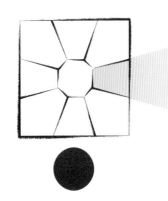

ELEMENT ■ METAL

I CHING TRIGRAM ■ LAKE

COMPASS DIRECTION ■ WEST

MOVEMENT OF CHI ■ INWARD

SHAPES ■ CIRCLES, OVALS, ARCHES, SPHERES

COLORS ■ GOLD, SILVER, WHITE, PASTELS

MATERIALS ■ METALS, METALLIC FINISHES, GEMS,
HARD STONE SUCH AS MARBLE AND GRANITE

IMAGERY ■ FLOWING, ROUNDED OBJECTS AND
IMAGES. OBJECTS RELATED TO CHILDHOOD.

Whether you have flesh-and-blood children in your home, or your "children" are your creative ideas and expressions, the Children and Creativity sector of the bagua influences both. In addition to decorating with objects to energize the powerful Metal element, curved lines and shapes help ideas flow easily and without resistance. Be sure to keep this sector tidy and well-maintained, or your thought patterns or children's behavior may reflect similar neglect or chaos.

146

TOOLS & MATERIALS

- 3 floral foam spheres*
- sheet of newspaper
- silver metallic spray paint
- used and/or broken compact discs, 6 to 10 CDs per sphere
- hot glue gun and glue sticks
- lengths of monofilament fishing line (optional)
- large needle or awl

* Available at craft stores. The spheres shown in the photo range from 6 to 8 inches (15.2 to 20.3 cm) in diameter.

CELESTIAL SILVER SPHERES

THESE ELEGANT REFLECTIVE SPHERES EMBODY THE ESSENCE OF METAL ELEMENT, AND IF YOU'RE LUCKY, THE RIGHT LIGHT ALSO CAUSES THEM TO PRODUCE A PRISMLIKE EFFECT OF RAINBOW COLORS. THE PROMOTIONAL COMPACT DISCS MASS-MAILED BY INTERNET SERVICE PROVIDERS MAKE EXCELLENT RAW MATERIAL FOR THIS PROJECT.

Designer ● Jodi Ford

INSTRUCTIONS

1 Working outdoors, lay the spheres on the sheet of newspaper. Spray-paint them silver and let dry.

2 Break the compact discs into clean, geometric shapes.

(Compared to irregular shapes, they're much easier to use when covering spheres.) Discard any pieces that contain printing or colors other than silver.

3 Hot glue disc pieces onto the surface of a sphere, fitting them as close together as you can until the entire surface is covered. Repeat with the other two spheres.

4 If you'd like to hang the spheres, use the needle or awl to make a hole in each sphere. Hot glue one end of a length of fishing line into each hole.

147

MARBLE-FACED GEM CLOCK

IN THIS PROJECT, YOU'LL TRANSFORM AN INEXPENSIVE PLASTIC WALL CLOCK INTO A SPARKLING BEAUTY. THE FACE IS MARBLEIZED WITH COLORFUL PASTEL PAINTS AND THE HOURS ARE POINTED OUT BY FACETED RHINESTONES. COLOR, GLITTER, AND MOVEMENT PROVIDE ALL THE THINGS THAT CHI LOVES.

Designer ● Lynn Krucke

INSTRUCTIONS

1 Carefully remove the front cover of the clock, then gently remove the hands and the paper face.

2 Use the paintbrush to coat the plastic clock case with leafing glue and let dry until the glue is tacky. Apply sheets of the silver leaf, covering all the glue-coated surfaces and pressing lightly to adhere the leaf.

3 Using the stencil brush, brush the leafed surface, burnishing the silver leaf onto the clock housing and removing excess leaf.

4 Cover the clock hands with the leafing glue and apply more silver leaf. Burnish, brushing away excess.

5 Following the paint manufacturer's directions, prepare the pan of water and drop the paints onto the water's surface. Use the toothpick to swirl the paints, creating a random pattern.

6 Carefully place the rice paper onto the water, transferring the swirled pattern to the paper.

7 Lay the paper flat to dry. If the paper curls while drying, it may be necessary to iron it flat before continuing.

8 Using the original paper face of the clock as a template, trace the face shape onto the marbled paper. Cut it out and make a hole at the center of the new face. Make light pencil marks at the three, six, nine, and twelve o'clock positions.

9 Glue the rhinestones onto the marbled paper face at the spots you marked. Let the glue dry.

10 Reassemble the clock and replace the cover.

TOOLS & MATERIALS

- **wall clock in plastic case**
- **paintbrush**
- **leafing adhesive (also called sizing glue)**
- **silver metallic composition leaf**
- **stencil brush**
- **shallow pan of water**
- **water-based marbling paints in pink, blue, yellow, and white**✲
- **toothpick**
- **rice paper in a size big enough to cover the clock face**
- **iron (optional)**
- **pencil**
- **scissors**
- **flat-backed rhinestones**
- **strong craft glue or epoxy**
- ✲ **Select the type that doesn't require thickeners for the water.**

Helpful People and Travel

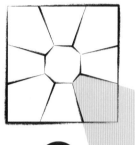

Element ▪ **Metal**

I Ching Trigram ▪ **Heaven**

Compass Direction ▪ **Northwest**

Movement of Chi ▪ **Inward**

Shapes ▪ **No fixed form**

Colors ▪ **Black, white, gray**

Materials ▪ **Metals and metallic finishes**

Imagery ▪ **Deities, angels, spiritual beings, mentors and teachers. Faraway places.**

Whether you have a desire to vacation at the beach or to make a pilgrimage to a holy place, the Helpful People and Travel sector of the bagua will support you. Items which evoke faraway places should go here, especially those made with Metal element. This sector contains predominantly masculine energy and also directs the energies of those who can be helpful to you. So place images of important deities, earthly benefactors, and inspirational mentors in this sector.

DOMESTIC SHRINE

IF THE HELPFUL BEINGS WHOSE ENERGY YOU'D LIKE TO TAP ARE DOMESTIC IN NATURE, THIS CHARMING SHRINE IS PERFECT FOR THAT SECTOR OF THE BAGUA. MADE OF BOLD, COLORFULLY LITHOGRAPHED FOOD TINS FROM ASIAN STORES, THE SHRINE ALSO REFLECTS A CONNECTION TO FARAWAY PLACES.

Designer ● Terry Taylor

TOOLS & MATERIALS

- 3 colorful tins, 1 large (a sesame oil can is perfect) and 2 small
- can opener
- work gloves
- flat metal file
- ruler
- black fine-tip permanent marker
- awl
- pop-rivet gun
- ¼-inch (6 mm) pop rivets
- flowers
- 2 votive candles and candleholders

INSTRUCTIONS

1 Remove one end of each can. To correctly orient the graphics of the candleholder portions of the shrine, open the bottoms of the two smaller cans, not their tops.

2 Empty the cans, discard the lids, and wash the cans thoroughly in soapy water. Carefully dry the cans.

3 Wearing the work gloves, use the file to smooth any jagged edges on the inner lips of the cans.

4 Measure and mark the positions of the candleholders.

Determine the best points to attach the candleholders to the can body, then use the awl to make small punctures in both at the points where they will be connected.

5 Holding a candleholder against the can body with the punctures aligned, insert a pop rivet through both punctures and use the pop-rivet gun to rivet them together.

6 Fill the can with flowers and set the votive candles on the candleholders. Remember, never leave a burning flame unattended.

Angel Wings Wall Altar

Wings, sky, and limitless vision: This altar perfectly embodies the energies of the Helpful People sector of a home. Add a small votive candle to the shelf if you wish, or use the mirror as the point of your meditative practice.

Designer ● *Sheri Bennett*

1 Photocopy the templates on pages 153 and 154, enlarging them as directed. Cut them out.

2 Place the templates on the MDF or wood and outline them with the pencil. Flip over the wing pattern to outline the second wing.

3 Use the jigsaw or saber saw to cut out the pieces: back arch, two wings, and shelf. Sand the edges to remove any roughness, and wipe them clean with the tack cloth.

4 If you'd like to add a hole for hanging the altar, measure to the center back of the arched piece and make a pencil mark. Using the router with the keyhole bit, make a hole at the mark. Or, after completing the altar, you may choose to install two eye screws on the back and add picture hanging wire.

5 Use the wood glue to glue the shelf to the bottom of the

arched piece, butting the bottom of the arched piece on top of the shelf. Nail into place. Let the glue dry.

6 Paint all the pieces with the light blue acrylic paint. Let dry, sand lightly, wipe clean with the tack cloth, and apply another coat of paint. Let dry. Paint small clouds on the arched back if desired. Let dry.

7 Use shades of white, pink, yellow to paint feathers on the sides of the wings that will face someone who views the altar. For an impressionistic, feathery effect, wet the brush and load it with all three colors, then follow the outline of the wing and pull up the brush, toward the top of the wing. Let dry.

8 Brush a coat of polyurethane over all the pieces. After applying it to the wings, quickly sprinkle on the glitter and sparkles before the wings dry.

9 Place the back and shelf assembly on a table, with the back flat

- **templates on page 153 and 154**
- **scissors**
- **¼- or ½-inch (6 mm or 1.3 cm) MDF board or wood, 15 x 24 inches (38.1 x 61 cm)**
- **pencil**
- **jigsaw or saber saw**
- **fine sandpaper**
- **tack cloth**
- **measuring tape**
- **router with keyhole bit (optional)**
- **wood glue**
- **1-inch (2.5 cm) finishing nails**
- **hammer**
- **paintbrushes**
- **acrylic paint in light blue, white, pink, and yellow**
- **clear acrylic polyurethane**
- **multicolored glitter and silver sparkles**
- **beveled mirror, 4 x 6 inches (10.2 x 15.2 cm)**
- **silicone glue**
- **15-inch (38.1 cm) piece of white fringe, 3 inches (7.6 cm) in width**
- **hot glue gun and glue sticks**
- **4 small gold hinges**
- **power screwdriver or drill**
- **picture hook**
- **2 eye screws (optional)**
- **picture-hanging wire (optional)**

ANGEL WINGS TEMPLATE 1
Enlarge 200%

against the table. Center the mirror on the back and mark its position. Use the silicone glue to adhere the mirror and let dry overnight.

10 Hot glue the fringe around the edge of the altar shelf, turning under a tiny margin at both ends.

11 Measure up 3¹/₂ inches (8.9 cm) from the bottom of the arched piece and mark the position of the hinges on both sides. Mark the position of the hinges on the wings. Screw in the hinges and hang the wings from the arched back piece so they "close" inward toward the mirror.

12 If desired, attach the eye screws and picture wire to the back and hang it from a picture hook.

ANGEL WINGS TEMPLATE 2
Enlarge 200%, then 11%

ANGEL WINGS TEMPLATE 3
Enlarge 200%, then another 200%

THE CENTER

ELEMENT ▪ EARTH

NO I CHING TRIGRAM

COMPASS DIRECTION ▪ CENTER

MOVEMENT OF CHI ▪ DOWNWARD

SHAPES ▪ LOW, FLAT, HORIZONTAL, SQUARE, RECTANGULAR, OCTAGONAL FORMS

COLORS ▪ YELLOWS, BROWNS

MATERIALS ▪ EARTH, STONES, CRYSTALS, POTTERY, CERAMICS, COTTON, SOFT STONES

IMAGERY ▪ LIMITLESS, OPEN SPACE

An open, uncluttered Center is essential to harmony and balance in the home, because all sectors of the bagua connect here. Any clutter or impediments will, in turn, hamper the free flow of the energies that support physical and psychic health. Decorations should be low, minimal, and supportive of the sector's Earth element, including the use of sand, soil, stones, or gems.

MANDARIN PATHWAY RUG

THIS RUG IS A CHARMING WAY TO ADD VISUAL INTEREST TO THE CENTER OF THE
BAGUA WHILE KEEPING IT OPEN AND UNCLUTTERED. YOU DON'T HAVE TO KNOW
HOW TO HOOK YARN OR BRAID RAGS TO MAKE IT, EITHER.

Designer ● Jane Wilson

1 Trim the upholstery fabric to the desired size, then follow the manufacturer's directions to use the iron-on adhesive hem tape to hem the raw ends.

2 After deciding the size, shape, and placement of the fabric "stones" that make up the pathway on the rug, cut out the stone shapes from the selected fabric, allowing a 1/2-inch (cm) margin. Fold under the margin of each stone and press with the iron.

3 Hot glue the stones to the rug, leaving a small opening in each. Insert stuffing in the openings to give the stones dimension, then hot glue them shut.

4 Now you'll create yarn "moss." Make moss tufts by wrapping the yarn around two or three fingers (fig. 1). Use more than one color of yarn in a tuft to achieve a more natural effect. Use a strand several inches or centimeters long to tie a knot at the bottom (fig. 2). Clip the other end of the bunch to free the strands of yarn (fig. 3). Put a dab of hot glue on each knot.

5 Hot glue the moss tufts to the rug, arranging them around the stones in a naturalistic pattern.

6 Pour the paint onto the plastic plate or dish, and lightly dip the sea sponge in the paint. Dab the sponge against the rug to remove excess, then apply the paint to the rug to give a mottled effect. (You may wish to experiment with a scrap of fabric first.) If the fabric has a nap, stroke the paint against the nap to preserve its texture. Let dry. Use several shades of paint to create a more natural look.

7 Spray the back of the rug with nonskid backing, or cut no-slip rug backing to fit. Lay the rug on top.

- **upholstery fabric with a nap, such as uncut corduroy or velvet, in an earthy brown or gold color**⁕
- **tape measure**
- **scissors**
- **iron-on adhesive hem tape**
- **1 to 2 yards (0.9 to 1.8 m) of fabric for stones, in contrasting earthy colors**
- **iron**
- **2 pounds (9.1 kg) of polyester fiberfill stuffing**
- **hot glue gun and glue sticks**
- **woolen yarn in several shades of earthy brown and gold**
- **acrylic paint in several shades of earthy brown and gold**
- **plastic plate or dish**
- **sea sponge**
- **clean rag or paper towels**
- **nonskid rug backing, either packaged by the roll or in spray-on form**

⁕ **Select fabric without a latex back. The rug shown measures 3 x 4 feet (0.9 x 1.2 m).**

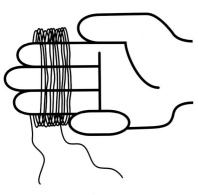

FIGURE 1

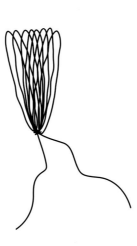

FIGURE 2

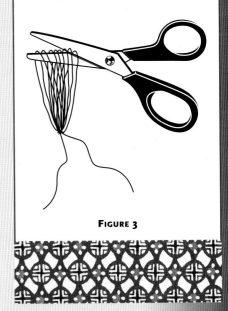

FIGURE 3

Acknowledgments

Sometimes the universe answers our needs in unexpectedly direct ways. I couldn't have written this book without the help of my new friend, Master Peter Leung, who showed good humor and great generosity in sharing his wisdom of many decades with me. Any errors in this book are strictly my own. Thanks are also due to my gifted art director Dana Irwin, assistant art director Hannes Charen, and to my other Lark colleagues Marcianne Miller and Rain Newcomb for their talented assistance, and to photographer Sandra Stambaugh for her beautiful and immaculate work.

Asheville, North Carolina is a community of people and places that help us connect with what some call God and some call Spirit, although that power transcends any name. Thank you to all the beneficent beings who helped with this book, including:

- Peter Alberice, Asheville, NC

- Kitty Brown of Sky People Gallery and Design Studio, 51 N. Lexington Avenue, Asheville 28801 (828) 232-0076

- Di Di Usha of Cosmic Vision, 34 N. Lexington Avenue, Asheville 28801 <www.cosmic-vision.com>

- Ariel and Quiana Ele'AnAriel of Essential Arts, 18 Wall Street, Asheville 28801

- Mark P. Fields of A Far Away Place, 11 Wall Street, Asheville 28801 (888) 452-1891

- Doctor Randall Johnson and Mary Johnson, Biltmore Forest, NC

- Ann Kaufmann of Dirt, 51 N. Lexington Avenue, Asheville 28801 (828) 281-DIRT

- Katie Skinner and Deedee Keasler of Loft, 53 Broadway, Asheville 28801 (828) 259-9303

I'd also like to thank our other friends around the world who contributed to this book, including:

- Bill Hocker, Hans-Georg Strunz, Jon Bower, Thomas Coxon, and Tracey Mackensie.

And let us not forget Kuan Kung, the Chinese god of literature, inspiration of ink-stained scribes everywhere.

Recommended Reading

Brown, Simon. *Feng Shui in a Weekend.* London: Hamlyn, 2002.

Brown, Simon. *Practical Feng Shui.* London: Ward Lock, 1997.

Collins, Terah Kathryn. *The Western Guide to Feng Shui Room by Room.* Carlsbad, California: Hay House, 1999.

Englebert, Clear. *Feng Shui Demystified.* Freedom, California: Crossing Press, 2000.

Stasney, Sharon. *Feng Shui Chic: Stylish Designs for Harmonious Living.* New York: Sterling Publishing Co., 2000.

Too, Lillian. *The Complete Illustrated Guide to Feng Shui.* Rockport, Massachusettes: Element, 1996.

Too, Lillian. *Essential Feng Shui.* New York: Ballantine Wellspring, 1998.

Too, Lillian. *The Illustrated Encyclopedia of Feng Shui.* Boston: Element, 1996.

Too, Lillian. *Lillian Too's Easy-to-Use Feng Shui.* London: Collins & Brown, 1999.

Wong, Eva. *Feng-Shui: The Ancient Wisdom of Harmonious Living for Modern Times.* Boston: Shambhala, 1996.

Photo Credits

Pages 6, 158, and 159:: Photographs courtesy of www.billhocker.com

Pages 10, 32: Black Box Photography, Asheville, NC; Steve Mann, photographer

Pages 12 (lower right), 14 (upper right): Apexphotos, Radley, Oxfordshire, England; Jon Bower, photographer <jon.bower@virgin.net> <www.apexphotos.com>

Page 13: Dragon illustration by Hans-Georg Strunz. Image courtesy of the Feng Shui Center Switzerland <www.fenshui-center.ch>

Page 15: Thomas Coxon Associates, Leicester, England; Sue Doughty, photographer <www.fengshui-consultants.co.uk>

Page 33: Tracey Mackenzie, Toronto, Canada, photographer <fengshuiforall.com>

IMAGE BY WWW.BILLHOCKER.COM

SHERI BENNETT, also known by her spiritual name of Sundara Fawn, began to express her deep passion for art in early childhood. Her work focuses on the interconnectedness of the individual and the universe and the spiritual light within each being. She offers special praise and thanks to her beloved master, Paramahamsa Yogananda, for the wisdom of his teachings. <sundara@tds.net> www.artnsoulonline.com

JODI FORD graduated with a BFA in illustration from The Savannah College of Art and Design, Savannah, Georgia. A freelance designer, she also works as an in-house graphic design and communications specialist at a community college. Her hobbies include Frisbee golf, rollerskating, and eating raisins and M&M candies.

ANGELA KILBY is a senior at the North Carolina School of Science & Math and was one of 52 students from the United States selected to attend the 2002 Research Science Institute at the Massachusetts Institute of Technology. Gifted in music as well as the sciences, she occasionally uses her talents to help out hapless right-brain craftspeople.

LYNN KRUCKE works with rubber stamps, paper, polymer clay, beads and wire, fabric, and fiber, and her favorite projects incorporate techniques from more than one medium. Lynn's designs have been featured in books on card making, beading, clocks, glass painting, candles, polymer clay, and wearable art. She lives in Summerville, South Carolina. <lkrucke@bellsouth.net>

MASTER PETER LEUNG has dedicated his life to the study of the ancient arts and sciences of China for the purpose of helping others to achieve good health and a better life. His expertise is derived from his personal research and his knowledge of rare classical texts. As a teacher and practitioner of the Chinese metaphysical arts and a director of the Feng Shui Association of Canada, Master Leung's guidance is sought by people from all walks of life, and he is honored to be considered a colleague by

great scholars in this field. His philosophy is to live with the Buddha in our hearts and to show compassion to all those in need. <fengshuisos.com>

TRACEY MACKENZIE is president of the Quebec Branch of the Feng Shui Association of Canada. She has studied Feng Shui for many years, most recently with Master Joseph Yu. She lectures extensively and has appeared on many television shows, including "Feng Shui Life." <traceym@feng-shuiforall.com>

JEAN TOMASO MOORE is a multimedia artist whose work has been featured in many Lark books. She and her husband live in the mountains of western North Carolina.

CATHY SMITH works in a variety of media. She is currently following her destiny in western North Carolina, accompanied and encouraged in this pursuit by husband, son, and assorted feline, canine, and reptilian family members.

TERRY TAYLOR lends his creative spirit full-time to Lark Books as a writer and designer. In his spare time, he creates and exhibits art in a variety of media. His designs have been featured in numerous publications.

JANE WILSON spent many years as a studio designer, after studying art history and design at East Tennessee University and technical drawing and drafting at Eastern Kentucky University. She is gifted in many media, including fiber arts, and lives in Black Mountain, North Carolina.

IMAGE BY WWW.BILLHOCKER.COM